Rhizomatic Reflections

Rhizomatic Reflections

Discourses on Religion & Theology

BAIJU MARKOSE

Foreword by Linda E. Thomas

WIPF & STOCK · Eugene, Oregon

RHIZOMATIC REFLECTIONS
Discourses on Religion and Theology

Copyright © 2018 Baiju Markose. All rights reserved. Except for brief quotations in critical publications or reviews, no part of this book may be reproduced in any manner without prior written permission from the publisher. Write: Permissions, Wipf and Stock Publishers, 199 W. 8th Ave., Suite 3, Eugene, OR 97401.

Wipf & Stock
An Imprint of Wipf and Stock Publishers
199 W. 8th Ave., Suite 3
Eugene, OR 97401

www.wipfandstock.com

PAPERBACK ISBN: 978-1-5326-3084-2
HARDCOVER ISBN: 978-1-5326-3086-6
EBOOK ISBN: 978-1-5326-3085-9

Manufactured in the U.S.A.   JANUARY 10, 2018

to
the little, little
resurrections of life

Unlike trees or their roots,
the Rhizome connects any point to any other point.

DELEUZE & GUATTARI, *A THOUSAND PLATEAUS*

Contents

Foreword by Linda E. Thomas | ix
Acknowledgments | xi
Introduction | xiii

Chapter 1   Planetary Conviviality: Celebration of Redeemed Relationalities | 1

Chapter 2   Church as the Coming Community: Expropriating Giorgio Agamben | 6

Chapter 3   Infinite Debt: Beyond Forgiveness | 12

Chapter 4   Black and White: Beyond the Binary, Lessons from Kelly Brown Douglas | 19

Chapter 5   The Problem of History and Taxonomy in *Sanskritic* Traditions | 34

Chapter 6   "Kammatipaadam" as Subaltern Sthala Purana: Dalit Spatial Discourses and Micro Eschatology | 44

Chapter 7   Re-Reading Ritual: Post-Enlightenment Theory and Subaltern Theology | 60

Chapter 8   Celebrating "Hybridity" and "Memory": Subaltern Religious Sensibilities in India | 72

CONTENTS

Chapter 9   "Sacred Grove": Reclaiming a Subaltern Paradigm for Ecological Restoration | 81
Chapter 10 Evolution as Grounding for Hospitality: Interfaith Interrogations | 97
Chapter 11 Eco-spiriting our Religious Philosophies: On Reviewing the Ecospirit | 111
Chapter 12 Reformation as 'Dangerous Memory': Re-membering an Unfinished Business | 116

Bibliography | *125*

Foreword

A PINNACLE OF MY journey as a professor has been the opportunity to work with a student as gifted as Reverend Baiju Markose. Such students are few, and as you read his essays, written as a doctoral student at the Lutheran School of Theology at Chicago, you will find that he is a person for all seasons. Like other great thinkers, Markose displays both precision in conceptualizing his ideas as well as remarkable theological imagination. You will find yourself turning pages quickly, looking forward to reading the next essay.

    I encourage all of my students to write for publication, but only a small few do, and of that small number, even fewer find publishers. I am thankful to Wipf & Stock for publishing this body of intellectually stimulating essays.

    I think of these essays as potent theological reflection on the notion of the rhizomatic, which as applied by Markose is a postcolonial move that takes us beyond the entrapment by Western binary perspectives to a more radical way of producing theological work. Drawing from Spivak's theory of alterity, as well as her foundational work as a postcolonial who questions history written by those who materially benefit from colonialism, Markose's intellectual work amassed in these essays draws upon his social location as a post-colonial, but from the perspective of those whose lives are marked by a caste system in India that profoundly de-privileges a particular group of people, Dalits. By bringing this particular perspective, Markose puts Spivak's work in check, as her postcolonial positionality is written from her social location as a Brahman. As a womanist anthropologist and theologian in the United States, I bring a perspective and sensitivity to what it means to do intellectual work from the perspective of those who have been historically oppressed by a capitalist society that gives ultra privilege to white people, especially white men. (White women benefit from the privilege white men have, as do their daughters and wives). The wealth factor is remarkable because people of African descent in the United States and Dalits in India are from lineages and ancestries that built the economy, infrastructure, and the very fabric of their respective nations (i.e., United States and India), including providing for the personal comfort of individuals with privilege, without being compensated one penny, nor given access to bases of power (e.g., elite schools, positions in government and business) in large numbers. This means that there is no intergenerational wealth passed onto the descendants of people of African descent in the United States, or to Dalits in India. This reality, in turn, affects accessibility to structural power that can shift law and order and all other matters having to do with the welfare of vulnerable people in each respective state.

Writing from the standpoint of a post-colonial intellectual who is a descendent of Dalits means that Markose (even with his male privilege), has lived and witnessed depravity existentially, and therefore has lived with those who embody and labor in a realm of radical rhizome—being free in unfree structures that impact everyday life. Each of the essays in this volume reach deeply into this zone and as such are an exceedingly important contribution to intersectional studies across disciplines, and are especially appropriate for those teaching and studying in theological settings.

Dr. Linda E. Thomas
Professor of Theology and Anthropology
Lutheran School of Theology at Chicago

Acknowledgments

NOTHING IS WRITTEN ALONE!
Everything is rhizomatically connected! I thank God for the beauty of interconnectedness of life; without that, my writing couldn't be possible. However, writing is a solitary experience for me through which I feel more healed and emplaced. It helps me to keep myself sharper, reflective, oriented, and attentive. Of course, it is not an effortless job for me. I thank God for the deadlines, friendly reminders, and positive anxieties which pushed me to the edge of creativity.

I thank Dr. Joseph Mar Thoma Metropolitan for granting me an excellent opportunity to study abroad. My sincere thanks to Dr. Isaac Mar Philoxenos Episcopa, the present diocesan bishop of North America-Europe Diocese of the Mar Thoma Church, who always encourages me to take up higher responsibilities.

I thank the Lutheran School of Theology community at Chicago, for instilling in me the unceasing academic fervor to do deeper search for Christian faith and praxis. Special thanks to my advisor Dr. Linda E. Thomas for blessing me with an insightful foreword for this book. Her academic caliber, social commitment, strong Christian faith, and divinely stimulated courage are always inspiring and challenging to me. Thanks to Dr. Vitor Westhelle, for enlightening me with sheer theological insights and

Acknowledgments

philosophical imaginations. Thanks to the faculty, colleagues, and friends in LSTC for their continuing support. I am indebted to Dr. Joe Mathew George and his family (Chicago Mar Thoma Church), who financially supported me to meet the expense of this publication effort. I thankfully remember the continuous support of the Mar Thoma Community in Chicago.

I cannot forget to say about the unending intimacy, love, and communion with my wife Stefi, my daughter Prarthana and my son Dhyan; without them, I would be deserted. I remember my mother Eleykkutty and my father, the late Mr. Markose, for they were the persons who impregnated my childhood with many poetic and prophetic imaginations. Finally, thanks to Wipf & Stock for bringing my thoughts into print.

Introduction

> She planted ambitious gardens.Before she left home for the fields, she watered her flowers, chopped up the grass, and laid out new beds.
>
> —ALICE WALKER[1]

FOR THE TITLE OF the book, I am indebted to the conceptual metaphor rhizome. This is an idea taken up by Deleuze and Guattari at the beginning of *A Thousand Plateaus*. The notion derails the modernist, linear thinking. Rhizome is a botanical term referring to a horizontal stem-like crabgrass that sends out roots and shoots from multiple nodes. It is not possible to locate a rhizome's source root. Rhizomatic thinking contrasts with *arborescent* (tree-like) thinking that develops from root to trunk to branch to leaf. According to Deleuze and Guattari, arborescent modes of thought are the characteristic of the grand narratives of modernist, capitalist thought. Deleuze and Guattari comment:

> We are tired of trees. We should stop believing in trees, roots, and radicals. They have made us suffer too much. All of *the arborescent* cultures is founded on them, from biology to linguistics. Nothing is beautiful or loving or

---

1. Walker, *In Search of Our Mother's Gardens*, 241.

Introduction

political aside from underground stems and aerial roots, adventitious growths, and rhizomes.[2]

The arborescent mode of thinking dominated in the western thought is hegemonic, as it naturalizes hierarchic orders by giving priority to narratives of origin. Rhizomatic thought proposes a non-hierarchy of multiple narratives without origin or central root to serve as the source. It discards the modern conceptions of human subjectivity. Instead of seeing human subjectivity as autonomous, individual entities like free-standing grass, rhizomatic thought looks at the human subjectivity regarding connectedness and heterogeneity. Deleuze and Guattari offer an example of the wasp and the orchid. Rather than describing each in the arborescent, hierarchical terminology of separate entities with distinct essences, Deleuze and Guattari require us to look at the interconnections, the points where the notion of individuality and essence breakdown. Therefore they say that "wasp and orchid, as heterogeneous elements, form a rhizome."[3] Rhizomatically, wasp, and orchid are interconnected each other. The wasp takes part in the reproductive process of orchid by transmitting pollen to it, and the orchid offers food for the wasp. In this interconnectedness between wasp and orchid, the boundaries are blurred. In summation, connections, heterogeneity, and multiplicity are the main thrust of rhizomatic thought. As Gordon Bearn observes, the rhizomatic thinking invites us to slow down and celebrate the interconnectedness.[4]

The essays in this book follow a rhizomatic pattern. They are heterogeneous but interconnected! They are horizontal, not vertical! They deal with a variety of themes in a trans-disciplinary fashion. All of these essays originated as the part of my PhD coursework in Lutheran School of Theology during the years of 2014–2016. Few of the essays came out of my special interest in the field of sociology, anthropology, and phenomenology of subaltern religion in India.

2. Deleuze and Guattari, *A Thousand Plateaus*, 15.

3. Ibid., 10.

4. Bearn, *Life Drawing: A Deleuzean Aesthetics of Existence*, 15.

INTRODUCTION

I attempted to integrate the Subaltern Theology with Subaltern Religion more precisely in those essays. But generally, this anthology spins around the issues of Casteism, Racism, Ecological Crisis, Globalization, Neoliberalism, and Resistance. And they are more suggestive than definitive. As they are suggestive, they are incomplete and imperfect. I consider incompleteness as an integral part of creativity! Finally, I would like to see this humble attempt as a part of a larger theopoetics of resistance.

Chapter 1

Planetary Conviviality
Celebration of Redeemed Relationalities

"Each of us is the destiny of the other."
—Jean Baudrillard[1]

WE ARE LIVING IN a world of exclusions. Exclusions abound from the supposed benign globalization on the one hand and various forms of militant reactionary movements on the other. The politics of fear and exclusion seem to be evident everywhere. An inevitable violence between the self and the other is assumed, which produces a proliferation of "gated" communities. The notion of "shrinking space" and "Global Village" has become an uncritical romanticization of the homogenizing tendency of the free market culture at the expense of the local and vernacular. Gayatri Chakravorty Spivak makes a distinction between the notion of "globe" and of "planet." Spivak lucidly puts it: "The globe is in our computer. No one lives there ... The planet is in the species of alterity, belonging to another system and yet we inhabit it, on loan."[2] Therefore, she

---

1. Baudrillard, *Impossible Exchange*, 84.
2. Spivak, *Death of a Discipline*, 72.

declares, "I propose the planet to overwrite the globe. Globalization is the imposition of the same system of exchange everywhere."[3]

What does it mean to be a human in this time of exclusion and violence, and what are the responsibilities endowed to us as Christians? Namsoon Kang, the famous diaspora theologian, asks: "What does it mean to continue to live as human, to remain faithful to the divine while living in a cultural, socio-geo-political, and religious world where power disparity between humans based on their nationality, citizenship, gender, race, class, ability, religion and so forth still prevails?"[4] Active Christian living, especially in the diaspora context, involves responding to these questions and stimulating the practice of freeing and enlarging human possibility in everyday realities. If loving one's neighbor as oneself, the core message of Christianity, is merely a spiritualized, romanticized rhetoric that people simply acquiesce to in the church without rigorously wrestling with the profound questions of the faith—such who is my neighbor, to whom am (are) I (we) neighbors, and what constitutes loving oneself and neighbors—then the significant value of loving one's neighbor as oneself loses its profound meaning. Based on the Spivakian idea of planetarity, Namsoon Kang proposes the idea of "Planetary Conviviality" as a paradigm for authentic Christian existence, witness and duty in a fragmented world like ours. Planetary conviviality emphasizes the responsibility to understand and to care for those who are on this planet as our fellow beings. The biblical idea of "the Kingdom of God" is proposed as the ethico-political and theological space of planetary conviviality. A few dimensions of this idea are expanded upon below.

---

3. Spivak, *Death of Discipline*, 72.
4. Kang, *Cosmopolitan Theology*, 181.

EPIPHANIES OF FACE

According to Immanuel Levinas, the ethical relation is fundamentally a "face-to-face relation."[5] The simple gaze at the face of the other beyond one's name, one's gender, and all other constructions, is transformative and divine. One's face precedes one's proper name and any kind of identity marker. There are several Biblical parallels for this sacred gaze at the face. It is in Jacob's gaze at the face of Esau (Gen 33:10) that Jacob realizes the "divine" on his face. The face was a sacred epiphany to Jacob. Jesus's gaze in the story of his encounter with Zacchaeus is another example. Jesus did not preach nor criticize him for being wrong. Instead, Jesus looked into Zacchaeus's face. When Jesus looked at his face, a miracle, an unexpected transformation, happened (Luke 19:2–10). For Zacchaeus, as a short person and tax collector, it must have been the first time in his lifetime that someone truly looked at his face without judgement—an embracing, affirming genuinely human gaze. What Jesus did was to look at the face of Zacchaeus, and Zacchaeus also was able to see the face of Jesus. There was no hierarchy of beings between these two faces. When Jesus calls his disciples at the beginning of John's gospel, the unconditional, face-to-face encounter leads to the act of following. Thus the primary responsibility of discipleship becomes facing the deep and the divine in the face of the other.

RADICAL HOSPITALITY

The event of a face-to-face encounter is liminal in character. No one could predict the actions of this event. In the Zacchaeus story, Jesus's first act was looking at Zacchaeus in his face, in which his first utterance was "I must stay at your house." There was no question of conditionality. The very liminal space between hospitality and hostility turns into the absolute willing of hospitality from both Jesus and Zacchaeus. Here the seemingly self-evident border between the host and the guest becomes blurry and is made

5. Levinas, *Difficult Freedom*, 22.

pointless through Jesus's act of traversing the border. Zacchaeus ultimately welcomes the uninvited visitation, and Jesus offers an invitation of himself to Zacchaeus. Jesus initiates moving beyond the rigid boundaries between the home, the host and the guest, and the borders between visitation and invitation. In this event, the absolute welcome of the epiphany happens in the face of the other. Abrahamic hospitality also serves as a paradigmatic illustration of radical hospitality in the unconditional welcoming of the epiphany of the face of strangers. As a host, Abraham bowed down to the ground (Gen 18:2) to welcome the faces of the three strangers, and then served the strangers water, bread, and meat. Without calculation or pondering their identity, Abraham offers hospitality to the guests. Planetary conviviality demands such radical hospitality, which goes beyond the hierarchy of host and guest. When there is no hierarchy of beings, there would be a genuine exchange of smiles and laughter. The song "Welcome Home," a celebrated song by New Zealand singer and songwriter Dave Dobbyn, rightly illustrates the notion of radical hospitality. Dobbyn was inspired to write the song after seeing Christchurch anti-racism protests and the sense of community that came through them. The song affirms an idea of radical hospitality: "I made a space for you."

REDEEMED RELATIONALITY

Radical hospitality redeems us to the point of celebrating our relationality and interconnectedness. The story of Zacchaeus ends with the affirmation of redeemed relationalities. Zacchaeus was inspired to celebrate redeemed relationality by exemplifying neighborly love, along with deep and radical compassion for fellow beings. Such reconfiguration of relationality is the central message of Christianity. In the *Coming of Cosmic Christ,* Mathew Fox calls us to reconfigure our relationship with the divine, fellow beings, and the mother earth.[6] Fox challenges us to enact the resurrection of the living Cosmic Christ in our beings, and then in our actions

---

6. Fox, *The Coming of the Cosmic Christ,* 13.

to transform society and bring healing to all the world's suffering, broken parts through the practices of love, imagination, peacemaking, and environmental, moral, and social justice. Fox argues that restoring the mystical mind of compassion, the Christian work of love, can bring a global renaissance to the entire world, including every aspect of society, from religion to sexuality, from peacemaking and disarmament to the mentoring of the youth. In conclusion, Fox calls for the celebration of redeemed relationality. Obviously, the remodeling and refashioning of the uneven world require planetary conviviality, the transformative love for the planet and planetary beings.

We celebrate planetary conviviality, not in a vacuum but community. The community is not a romanticized imaginative space, but a realistic, challenging space where we lose ourselves to find ourselves more meaningfully. Jean Vanier says that "Community is a terrible place. It is the place where our limitations and our egoism are revealed to us. When we begin to live full-time with others, we discover our poverty and weaknesses, our inability to get on with people, our mental and emotional blocks, our seemingly insatiable desires, our frustrations and jealousies, our hatred and our wish to destroy. While we were alone, we could believe we loved every one. Now that we are with others, we realize how incapable we are of loving, how much we deny life to others."[7] Being in the community always demands a re-positioning of ourselves for the betterment of the community. Planetary conviviality is such a revolutionary mode of understanding and reconfiguring the self, the others and the world. It is an ethic of responsibility, compassion, hospitality, as well as an ongoing exercise of interdependence in the face of violence, war, and exclusion. In the light of planetary conviviality, I would like to re-define "church" as the community which happens in an amazing serendipitous way in the midst of our everyday life with its complexities. The church is a wonderful space, where we celebrate the epiphany of marginal faces, radical hospitality, and redeemed relationality through the paradigm of Jesus Christ.

---

7. Vanier, *Community and Growth*, 17.

Chapter 2

Church as the Coming Community
Expropriating Giorgio Agamben

"The coming being is whatever being."[1]

—Giorgio Agamben

UNDENIABLY AGAMBEN IS A prominent figure in Continental Philosophy. His work is multifaceted and elaborative. He uses many resources which dissolve the traditional disciplinary borders. Agamben's thought world is highly resistant to any "reductionist representations or labels."[2] His conceptual world is anchored in the distinction between the "*Bios*" and "*Zoe*,"[3] i.e. the political and nonpolitical life. *Bios* is the life in the city (*polis*), and *Zoe* is the bare life that humans have simply as themselves. How do both of these realms relate and interact each other? What is the role of sovereign power in this dialectic? These are the primary concerns for Agamben. "The Coming Community" is a significant work in

---

1. Agamben, *The Coming Community*, 1.
2. Dickinson, *Agamben and Theology*, 2.
3. Agamben, *Homo Sacer*, 1.

which Agamben describes the socio/political/ethical implications of his philosophical thought. In "Coming Community," Agamben introduces the concept of "whatever singularity," the core idea behind his philosophical inquiries on the theme "community." The concept of "whatever singularity" has an uncanny parallel with the concept of 'liminality' that developed by Victor Turner.

WHATEVER SINGULARITY

The book "Coming Community" begins with a messianic overtone by stating "the coming being is whatever being."[4] The translator immediately gives an explanation of the Italian root word; *qualunque*,[5] in the footnote. The Italian "*qualunque*" is poorly translated as "whatever" in English. The word "whatever" refers to "pure indifference" in the sense "whatever, it doesn't matter." But in Latin, it has a diagonally opposite meaning: "what always matter." For Agamben, it is "what always matter," regardless of whatever it is. It is lovable and desirable. Agamben defines "whatever singularity" as a unique singularity which a lover finds in his/her lover. He says;

> Love is never directed toward this or that property of the loved one (being blond, being small, being tender, being lame), but neither does it neglect the properties in favor of an insipid generality (universal love): The lover wants the loved one with all of its predicates, it's such as it is . . . Thus, whatever singularity (the lovable) is never the intelligence of something, of this or that quality or essence, but only the intelligence of an intelligibility.[6]

The Pauline usage of the term "whatever" is noteworthy. Paul repeatedly uses the word to refer to the cardinal Christian virtues. "Finally, brothers and sisters, *whatever* is true, *whatever* is noble, *whatever* is right, *whatever* is pure, *whatever* is lovely, *whatever* is admirable—if anything is excellent or praiseworthy—think about

---

4. Agamben, *The Coming Community*, 1.
5. Ibid., 107.
6. Ibid., 2.

such things" (Phil 4:8, italics added). Paul exhorts the church at Philippi, after discussing the Christian desire for a resurrected life / heavenly citizenship / transcendent life (Phil 3:10–21), as he was doing the same. For Paul, Christians are those who consider "resurrection" as an every day / every moment practice (Col 3:1). He considers this "resurrection" as a resurrection into the *Zoetical* life. Paul uses the word "Zoe" repeatedly in Phil 1:20, 2:16, 4:3, and 4:8, with the meaning "absolute fullness of life" or "the state of one who is possessed of vitality." Thus the Pauline "whatever" refers to an essential quality of a resurrected being. So, one can conclude that the "whatever being" is a resurrected being and the resurrected being is a "whatever being." Two relevant dimensions of "whatever singularity" are being discussed below.

Non-Representability

Unlike other continental philosophers, Agamben doesn't negate the dichotomies; but he turns them inside-out and points to space where they become indistinguishable. This is an important shift characterized by Agamben's philosophy. This "indistinguishability" is embodied in the concept of "whatever singularity." For Agamben, this is the focal point. He reminds again and again that the concept of "whatever singularity" surpasses the choice between particular and universal, common and proper, genus and individual, inside and outside, potentiality and actuality, etc. Hence, it is important to note that the "whatever singularity" is beyond such binary oppositions. It is beyond any bracketing or the normalizing tendencies of the sovereign. This singularity is already there with the collective, the people. This collective dimension is unyielding in Agamben. And this "collective whatever singularity" is beyond any normalization. The attribute of "non-representability" is not strictly "static" in essence, but it is an "infinite series of modal oscillations."[7]

---

7. Ibid., 19.

Potentiality

Another critical dimension of "whatever singularity" is its "Potentiality." Agamben takes the Aristotelian concept of dialectics between potentiality and actuality as the base. According to Agamben, the decisive characteristic of potentiality is "the potentiality to not be."[8] "Whatever being" is potential, not regarding its capability "to be," but regarding its capability "to not be." The capability to "not be" is that which makes the singularity. A new reading of *kenosis* (Phil 2:5–11) is possible here. In a way, the "impotentiality" becomes the heart of "potentiality." William Watkin rightly observes that "for Agamben, impotentiality is not weakness but the origin of real strength."[9] This "potentiality to suspend" is messianic in character. Here it is worthy to note the Pauline usage of the phrase *hos me* ("as not") is connected to the idea of potentiality. Agamben uses two words intertextually, namely *klesis* ("vocation") and *hos me* ("as not") (1 Cor 7:29–32). *Hos me* is the formula concerning messianic life, and it is the ultimate purpose of *klesis*;[10] it means to sustain in the vocation in a special way of being "as not." In this sense, Agamben interprets Paul's use of these phrases from an Indian philosophical sensibility of "detached attachment." According to Andrew Robinson, this Agambenian stance is almost similar to the "Buddhist stance of contemplative separation which preserves instead of deciding."[11]

COMING COMMUNITY: THE "COLLECTIVE WHATEVER SINGULARITY."

The Agambenian idea of community traverses any traditional essentialist concepts of community. For Agamben, the "coming community" is the "collective whatever singularity." The "collective"

---

8. Agamben, *The Coming Community*, 35.
9. Watkin, *Agamben and Indifference*, 95.
10. Agamben, *The Time That Remains*, 23.
11. Robinson, "In Theory Giorgio Agamben: Destroying Sovereignty," para. 5.

doesn't refer to any belongingness or representation (e.g., being red, Indian, French, or activist). It is a belonging without claiming any "essential" or "foundational" identity. For Agamben, the "coming community" is an *apophatic* community which is beyond any representation. This means that it is a negative community based on "whatever singularities" counterposed to the sovereignty. Agambenian community exists simply to be, "such as it is."[12] It is beyond any static institutionalized forms. It doesn't use traits of identity to distinguish itself from the "other." "Agambenian community" is marked with its non-representability.

CHURCH AS THE "COMING COMMUNITY."

We are living in a world of exclusions. The disconnect between the "self" and "other" has triggered a culture of fear and produced "gated communities." An inevitable violence of exclusion within the human existence is being taken for granted. In this context, the Agambenian idea of "whatever singularity" challenges us to redefine *ecclesia* as the "collective whatever singularity." Gordon Zerbe is very apt when he interprets "coming community" from an ecclesiological perspective: "Agamben's Ecclesia is an abstract aggregate of messianic callings."[13] The coming community is a spontaneous social togetherness beyond any representation, and it is apocalyptic in nature. Turner's concept of *communitas* also points to this dimension of the spontaneity of social togetherness. In this light, I would like to redefine church as a "coming community," which happens in an amazing, serendipitous way, in our everyday life through the paradigm of Jesus Christ. It is a creative space for celebrating radical hospitality and redeemed relationality. Let me conclude with the words of Agamben, reminding us how revolutionary "whatever singularity" in its "potentiality" is: "Whatever singularity, which wants to appropriate belonging itself, its being in language, and thus rejects all identity

12. Agamben, *The Coming Community*, 1.
13. Harink, *Paul, Philosophy, and the Theopolitical Vision*, 8.

and every condition of belonging, is the principal enemy of the state. Wherever these singularities peacefully demonstrate their being in common, there will be a Tiananmen, and sooner or later, the tanks will appear."[14]

---

14. Agamben, *The Coming Community*, 87.

Chapter 3

Infinite Debt
Beyond Forgiveness

"There is a difference between having debt and being indebted."[1]
—Amaryah Shaye

We live in an age of the infinite debt. The growing dominance of finance capital governs our everyday life and practices. As Maurizio Lazzarato has argued,

> With the proliferation of credit, and with the enforced reliance on credit because of the declining purchasing power of wages and other forms of economic immiseration, we have witnessed the creation of "indebted man," a new kind of subjectivity which can be trusted to expend itself in continually paying back.[2]

This new kind of subjectivity has constructed in a mode of infinite indebtedness. In this context, we might ask about the purported radicality of the language of the gift, including the forgiveness of debt, in the Christian tradition. The connection between debt

1. Shaye, "Blackness and Value," para. 1.
2. Lazzarato, *The Making of the Indebted Man*, 162.

forgiveness and Jubilee themes in Biblical traditions remind us of the subversive nature of debt forgiveness. But is forgiveness indeed subversive? Or does it indeed perpetuate indebtedness by maintaining the debtor-creditor relation? Who exercises the power of agency in the debt forgiveness? Where are the darker bodies positioned in this power relation? And how do we uncover the revolutionary potentiality of forgiveness from the standpoint of the debtor? These are some crucial questions that we need to ask in the neoliberal economic context today.

GENEALOGY OF DEBT

A genealogy of the concept of debt will give us more light into its complexity. In the second essay of *The Geneology of Morals*, Nietzsche researches the connection between debt and the eternal sense of obligation that comes from an internalized feeling of guilt. But what is the force that internalizes guilt? It is a fear of violent repercussions, driven by the memory of pains suffered. Where does this come from? Nietzsche argues that it comes from a particular, primitive social relation: the debtor-creditor relation, in which the creditor extracts pain and suffering from the debtor in the penalty for their non-payment. Punishment is an intrinsic feature of the debt-creditor relation.[3] Debt, in effect, yields a fear of punishment, which is internalized as guilt. The alliance of this "guilt" with the classical Christian theories of atonement cannot be bypassed. According to St. Anselm (*Cur Deus Homo*), the sinful human beings have offended God's honor, and are thus liable for the debt of honor that they have incurred. Interestingly, this debt is not payable for two reasons: first, it could only be paid by offering a surplus of honor to God, but that is not possible because they already owe God perfect obedience; and second, because the debt that they have incurred is infinite, and infinite debt can never be settled by people with finite resources. This "infinite debt" conscience is the one of the pivotal affirmation of Christianity until

---

3. Nietzsche, *On the Genealogy of Morals*, 63.

now. By indoctrinating an ontological guilt consciousness, Christianity endorsed infinite debt of the neo-liberal ecosystem.

The sustenance of infinite debt exercised through inventing sovereign powers—this is how neoliberalism works now. Bruce Rogers-Vaughn keenly observes, "Neoliberalism is both a form of hegemonic control that serves the interests of financial elites and a form of governance that adapts to local circumstances and shapes individual subjects and their personal relationships."[4] Vaughn goes further in analyzing the manifestation of this economic hegemony. He states: "Hegemony is a tricky concept and provokes muddled thinking. No project achieves 'hegemony' as a completed project. It is a process, not a state of being."[5] The economic hegemony, as a process, maintains itself by creating indebtedness as social debt, which has so many ramifications, especially for the black and brown bodies.

ECOLOGY OF THE CAPITAL

As Shaye suggests, we must think about the financial capitals ecologically.[6] By ecology, it refers to the social relations that enable the invention and maintenance of the capitals. The ecology of neoliberal capitals must be problematized in the light of racism. Amaryahshaye uncovers the unholy alliance between global financial capital and racial capital. She analyzes the construction of the idea, "whiteness as credit and blackness as debit" in the context of global capitalism. The global capitalism came into being and expansion with the invention of racism. Shaye builds upon Philip Goodchild's formulation that the promise of value offered by the global capitalism is dependent on the promise of debt. She observes,

> The promise of value is dependent on the promise of debt—the promise that the black will never be able to repay its debts and that the overwhelming debt accrued by

---

4. Rogers-Vaughn, *Caring for Souls in a Neoliberal Age*, 55.
5. Ibid.
6. Shaye, "Blackness and Value," para. 4.

blackness will be what organizes the principle of money's promise. A permanent indebtedness, then, is the condition of blackness.[7]

Blackness is not recognizable apart from the imposition of a permanent indebtedness. On the other hand, whiteness is only recognizable as being separate from its debts. This type of "credibility" towards whiteness and "indebtedness" towards blackness is extended, circulated, and maintained for the sake of global capitalism. Thus blackness and brownness become the demarcations of exclusion from the customary social relations promoted by the new credit/debit system.

FORECLOSURE OF THE FUTURE

The problem with credit and debit in a neo-liberal context is that it delimits our vision. It consciously constructs an economic/political/social condition in which debt is considered as the horizon and limit of thought. Debt mediates our sense of time, creating a past that starts at the moment of becoming a debtor and that flows into a future that has been foreclosed. Debt, in many ways, is the possession of the future in advance by objectifying it. Possessing in advance means subordinating all possibility of choice and decision in the future. Thus the neoliberal credit/debit economic system becomes a device of foreclosure—as Maurizio Lazzarato argues, a foreclosure of the future.[8] To be bred into predictability means that the capacity to surprise, even to create, is bred out of us. We are compelled to act in ways that are determined by our obligations from the past, and time itself becomes a commodity that is captured and exploited; therefore, we never have a future that is more than a bare repetition of the past. We get up. We go to work. We make our payments. And then do it all again.

---

7. Ibid.
8. Lazzarato, *The Making of the Indebted Man*, 46.

BEYOND FORGIVENESS

Here we need to revisit the relation of Christianity to debt, paying special attention to Jesus's treatment of the problem of debt. To uncover the genuinely subversive element in Jesus's teaching requires seeing such texts as the Lord's Prayer, not as regarding a principle of debt forgiveness, but as abolishing the debtor/creditor relation. Does Christian tradition offer any resources for resisting infinite debt, especially since it has been a contributing factor to it? The Lord's Prayer in the Gospel of Matthew, Chapter 6, contains the line: "Forgive us our debts, as we forgive our debtors." As New Testament scholars have pointed out, Jesus here picks up on Hebrew tradition of "Jubilee," which periodically would have erased long-standing debts that produced massive inequalities and sometimes reduced people to peonage. In Jesus's time, this was a live issue, because urban-based land owners around 20 CE accumulated surplus wealth from occasional bumper crops and sought ways to invest. They did this by making loans to peasants, who lived hand to mouth. Upon contracting loan obligations, a cycle of indebtedness ensued which often led to default.

In addition to the personal and family crises generated by these conditions, there was a more pervasive and enduring form of debt that also preserved and exacerbated unequal conditions among Jesus's hearers. As John Dominic Crossan observes, Jesus's aim in this prayer and throughout much of his ministry was the dismantling of the honor system characteristic of Judean/Galilean society. Debt forgiveness meant liquidation of what we might call social capital. This entails the abolition of the system of finite debts characteristic of archaic societies in general, but also of the finite debt generated by the Roman empire which they owed the Eastern Mediterranean. Forgiveness of debt means the refusal of patronal relations, even to the empire.

The limitation of forgiveness is that it preserves the creditor/debtor relation, even in abolishing the debt. What is needed, instead, is liberation or release from debt. The difference between forgiveness and liberation is in the object: forgiveness is of the debt while preserving the creditor/debtor relation, while liberation is from the relation itself. Thus, only the latter attacks the imbalance of power that infinitely generates doubt. We see this drive toward liberation in the structure of the Lord's Prayer that situates the one who prays between forgiving and being forgiven. The hierarchical power relations that are structured into the debt system offer both benefit and burden to those whose role is inscribed in the system. To be liberated from the system, one has to be enabled to refuse both. For all of the complications and dangers that it involves, this vision of liberation from debt has the advantage of stressing the agency of indebted persons, who destroy the system of debt insofar as they achieve collective action: a collective refusal and collective construction of an alternative system of non-exploitative social credit. The plural first-person pronoun here is crucial: liberation can only be an act of the "we." The "we" factor in the Lord's Prayer points to the communitarian dimension of the people's resistance.

Community, Immunity, and Biopolitics

The widow's mite can be taken as another biblical metaphor to deconstruct the mode of economic practice. Calling his disciples to him, Jesus said, "Truly I tell you, this poor widow has put more into the treasury than all the others" (Mark 14:43). Here Jesus re-evaluates the Roman imperial economic practices by reclaiming the economic credibility (not the indebtedness) of the excluded: the widow. Widows, orphans, and foreigners were considered indebted, at the margins of the imperial economic-political system. The brave and intentional act of this widow in Mark can be taken as a symbolic political act of dismantling the creditor/debtor economic system in the ancient Near-East, which used to keep widows as eternally indebted. The act also reimagines the agency of the little ones, the excluded.

The agency of the indebted should be reclaimed. Shaye points to a kind of collective movement from the side of black and brown bodies, who are excluded, criminalized by the current credit-debit economic system. She says that

Rhizomatic Reflections

> ... To transgress the limit of debt, to inhabit the space where the indebted have been living their non-credible criminal lives, is to make a move that reevaluates the value money promises.[9]

This is a call to have a new sense of community preserving an immunity towards violent economic practice based on a new *biopolitics*[10] grounded on life (*Bios*) not on death (*Thanatos*).

---

9. Shaye, *Blackness and Value*.
10. Esposito, *Terms of the Political*, 110.

Chapter 4

Black and White
Beyond the Binary, Lessons from Kelly Brown Douglas

"In a dualistic relationship mutuality of difference is precluded."[1]

KELLY BROWN DOUGLAS

IN HER BOOK *WHAT'S Faith Got to Do with It? Black Bodies/ Christian Souls,* Kelly Brown Douglas delineates the theoretical roots of black slavery. She finds that Platonization of Christianity played a major role in legitimizing slavery. The body-soul divide of Platonized Christianity naturally equated with white/black antagonism. This concept of binary opposition was fueled by the Enlightenment tradition, which placed reason over passion. Even the evangelical Protestant faith has played a critical function in legitimizing slavery by putting individual souls over bodies. But the black people were not just passive recipients of Platonized Christianity; they appropriated the Christian faith and made it meaningful. There may be many dispositions of Platonic tradition in black

---

1. Douglas, *What's Faith Got to Do with It?: Black Bodies/Christian Souls,* 19.

faith, but it was not a blind adaptation. Through the hermeneutics of appropriation, black people were able to make Christianity relevant to them. According to Douglas, the hermeneutics of appropriation and the core theological themes of black faith were reclaimed (retrieved) by womanist theological expressions. Through these theoretical engagements, Douglas tries to explain a crucial question: how one can be a Christian and a woman? To explore the roots of the legitimization of black slavery, Douglas refers to its theoretical underpinnings. The attack against the black body is the result of "antagonistic dualistic paradigms"[2] created by Platonic/Stoic thought and its coalition with Christianity. The Enlightenment tradition has also influenced much in the demonization of the flesh/body along with white cultural ideology.

PHILOSOPHICAL/IDEOLOGICAL ROOTS OF PLATONIZED CHRISTIANITY

The interplay between Platonized Christianity and white cultural ideology made slavery comfortable. These influences constructed blacks as something innately irrational and inferior. We can trace its moorings to the binary opposite notions of the Enlightenment and Platonism discourses. The reasoning ability which connects with soul and mind has virtually divinized. But the passion ability which combines with the body has been devalued. "White" is considered as something innately rational and sound, while "black" is something irrational and evil. These theoretical equations made black enslavement a divinely ordered concept. Moreover, Douglas points to an important conceptual necessity to explore Christianity's compatibility with two dominant oppressive cultural narratives: 1) the Enlightenment narrative on "reason," and 2) white cultural constructions of "blacks." She says that "Platonized Christianity with the influence of Enlightenment rationality provided

---

2. Ibid., xv.

a 'sacred canopy' for both white cultural ideology and scientific racism."[3]

This "sacred canopy" represents the continued violence against the black body sanctioned by Enlightenment discourse, white cultural ideology, and Platonized Christianity. It is a complex social reality. The theoretical roots of these three discourses are based on the concept of body-soul/mind antagonism. Let us further explore the role of these three discourses.

Platonic/Stoic Influence

When we study early Christian formation from the first centuries, the Hellenistic influence is very evident. The ideas of Philo, Seneca, and Plato significantly influenced Christian thought. Douglas prefers to coin this influence "Hellenized religion."[4] In this Hellenized religion, Platonic thought played a major role. The theory of two different spheres of existence is the core of Platonism. The "world of Forms" is the realm of the transcendent, immaterial, and unchangeable. The "world of Senses" is the realm of material and the changeable, and is in direct opposition to the "world of Forms" because they are mutually opposite in nature. Here we see an apparent dualistic tendency in Platonism. The spaciotemporal changing reality of material (world of Senses/Matter) is inferior to the spiritual reality of ideas, while the unchanging (world of Forms/Spirit) is superior. That means the spirit is something superior to matter. Frank Thilly opines that the core argument of Platonism is that "Man is composed of material body and spiritual, eternal soul, and the reality is soul alone."[5] The privilege of one reality over the other is the tyranny of Platonic dualism.

Dualistic epistemology is the core of Platonism. It suggests an array of dualistic hierarchies, to interpret the reality. It is evident that going higher in the Platonic hierarchy means becoming purer.

---

3. Douglas, *What's Faith Got to Do with It?*, 132.
4. Ibid., 24.
5. Thilly, *A History of Philosophy*, 75.

Another important Hellenistic influence is Stoic thought, which significantly affected Christianity. Stoicism rejected the Platonic disregard for the material world. The Stoic concept of "ideal living" (*Apatheia*) suggests a living free from passion and guided by reason. It is an idea of living without worldly and bodily desires.

Both of these philosophies highly regard reason over passion. According to Platonism and Stoicism, human life should be by the rational principle, which is antagonistic to what is bodily. The Platonic and Stoic philosophies suggest a dualistic understanding of reality. They place the divine/transcendent as the polar opposite of the mundane/human. This worldview has negatively influenced Christian theology by conceptualizing the body as something to be innately devalued.

The Enlightenment Influence

The eighteenth-century European intellectual movement is known as the Enlightenment, and is defined by historians as a project of modernity. Regarding the understanding of the body, modernity constructed a philosophy of mind-body dualism in continuation with Platonic dualism. Paulose Mar Gregorios, in his famous work entitled *A Light Too Bright*, criticizes the project of modernity. He says that "the modern notion of separative self-desacralized nature has resulted in the marginalization of the people who lived in a symbiotic relationship with nature and rejected their knowledge as irrational and unscientific."[6] The problem is that the Enlightenment rationality presupposed a "disembodied"[7] subject. That means it rejected embodied experiences. Thus it presupposed that bodily activities are secondary, while mental thoughts are primary. This also resulted in a dualistic epistemology based on the mind-body divide. Douglas says that

---

6. Mar Gregorios, *A Light Too Bright*, 29.

7. Disembodiment means placing human subject above the influence of the world, unaffected by it. Embodiment means to be influenced, affected, and conditioned by history. See Falzon, *Foucault, and Social Dialogue: Beyond Fragmentation*, 26.

... In many respects, owing to the spirit of the enlightenment, science fueled and kept alive the vital ideology necessary for white exploitative abuse of the black body. The vitality of white culture is thus in many respects a legacy of the Enlightenment secreted by the scientific racism that provided a rational canopy for white supremacist practices.[8]

White Cultural Ideology

Douglas examines the link between white cultural ideology and Platonized Christianity. The underlying assumption of her argument is that eighteenth-century Enlightenment discourse provided the essential meta-narrative that stimulated the bond between white culture and Platonized Christianity, which worked to legitimize black slavery. In legitimizing slavery, white cultural ideology and Enlightenment discourse join together. Douglas shrewdly observes that "the defining principle of white supremacist ideology is the hyper-bestial sexuality of black women and men."[9] Additionally, the caricatures of black people as oversexed have allowed the black body to be continually controlled and exploited by white supremacists. However, two important things should be noted here: one is "control" and the other is "profit." The notion of black women and men as sex objects also helped white people substantiate their control over the black body, with significant monetary benefits (profit) for them. All of these oppressive structures were fashioned in ways that have benefited a white racist society.

PLATONIZED CHRISTIANITY AS HERESY

Douglas identifies Platonized Christian tradition as heretical, primarily because of its compatibility with the dominant white cultural ideology. Platonized Christianity must reject the doctrine of

---

8. Douglas, *What's Faith Got to Do with It?*, 119.
9. Ibid., 114.

incarnation itself. Its alliance with an unjust power (racism) makes the existential reality of incarnation dangerous. So Platonized Christianity can be considered as "dangerous as it is heretical."[10] Further, "Christianity's alliance with Platonic/Stoic thought was the primary troubling association that laid the foundation for a terrorizing Christian legacy about the black body."[11] Douglas says "Platonized Christianity has generated 'dualistic epistemologies' and ways of relating. Christian participation in vicious attacks on the black body reflects this tradition."[12]

The Problematic Theological Core

Douglas identifies two questionable theological cores that are important in Platonized Christianity. They are closed monotheism and Christological paradox. The Hellenistic influence through Platonic/Stoic ideas and the Hebrew belief of a "chosen people" have all molded Christianity into a monistic ideal. The idea of a chosen people automatically presupposes that there is an "other" who has not been selected. Most often this other is considered as "pagan" or, in this instance, "black." So Douglas calls this type of closed monotheism something "inherently antagonistic."[13] She says,

> The antagonistic/oppositional propensity that is natural to a closed monotheism portends a troubling reality. One can already begin to see from this single theological claim of Christianity the underpinnings of a terrorizing Christian Tradition.[14]

Regarding the Christological paradox of Platonized Christianity, Douglas problematizes the Christological debate on divinity and humanity. The Councils of Nicea and Chalcedon helped the early church to define the divinity vs. humanity relationship

10. Douglas, *What's Faith Got to Do with It?*, 149.
11. Ibid., xv.
12. Ibid., 20.
13. Douglas, *What's Faith Got to Do with It?*, 14.
14. Ibid., 15.

of Jesus. The councils affirmed the full humanity and full divinity of Jesus. In essence, two different natures (divinity and humanity) have come together. The Christological argument naturally ends with the idea of an ontological paradox. According to Douglas, it is problematic to imagine a twofold paradox in Christology. A paradox doesn't point to dualism, but it can be easily interpreted as dualistic opposites. Douglas comments that "there has been an influential, oppressive Christian tradition that has generated dualistic epistemologies . . . Christian participation in vicious attacks on black bodies reflects this tradition."[15]

Platonized Discourse on Sexuality

Platonized Christianity has also demonized sexuality. The interpretation of sexuality as sin is reinstated by Augustinian and Pauline thoughts. Sex for any purpose other than procreation is seen as ungodly, and the people who practice it are deemed to be sinners. This is a concept deeply rooted in Platonized dualism, which strongly promotes the soul-body dichotomy. Moreover, this interpretation of sex and sexuality has become a useful tool in the hands of the powerful. Therefore, Douglas suggests that Platonized Christian discourse on sexuality must be placed at the table with the discourses of power. Douglas uses Foucauldian analysis of sexuality and power to explain its complexity: "Sexuality is a mechanism by which distinctions can be made between classes and groups of people."[16] Platonized Christianity has interpreted that sexually driven people are ungodly and enemies of God. This interpretation has naturally legitimized the attacks of whites on the black body. To demonstrate that black people are hypersexual creates control over them, which can be interpreted as a power play of the dominant whites.

The direct victim of Platonized discourse on sexuality is none other than the black woman's body. The body of black women has

15. Ibid., 20.
16. Ibid., 51.

long been described as bestial, and lust-ridden. Black women have been labeled as "Jezebels" in another attempt at control and exploitation by the dominant whites. For this reason, Douglas calls for liberation from these dualistic dispositions, through authentic womanist expressions.

Platonized Protestantism

The Protestant tradition was also unable to distance itself from this Platonic influence. A close analysis of protestant spirituality details a strong influence of Platonic dualism. The spirit of individualistic salvation, purity, commitment, hard work, etc. also changed the larger European society during the eighteenth and nineteenth centuries. Max Weber notes the varying effects of Protestant spirituality in the development of modern capitalism. He says,

> But not all the Protestant denominations seem to have had an equally strong influence in this direction. That of Calvinism, even in Germany, was among the strongest, it seems, and the reformed faith more than the others appears to have promoted the development of the spirit of capitalism, in the Wupperthal as well as elsewhere.[17]

For Max Weber, the protestant ethics that based on purity, salvation, and asceticism promoted the capitalist spirit that emerged in Europe. Also, in America, Protestantism had a growing role, particularly among evangelical Protestants. Evangelical Protestantism was very influential in America during the eighteenth and nineteenth centuries. Many black people were quickly attracted by the Protestant Pietism and began to practice this form of Christianity. Protestantism allowed blacks to exercise their traditional black expressions from their African contexts, and for this reason, blacks and Protestantism became quickly compatible.

---

17. Weber, *The Protestant Ethic and the Spirit of Capitalism*, 10.

Platonic Dispositions in Protestantism

Evangelical Protestantism became more influential in America during the Great Awakenings of the eighteenth and nineteenth centuries. Despite being rooted in a Platonic dualistic epistemology, it still provided a space for black faith affirmations and traditions. In several ways, it was a Platonized Christianity. Douglas opines that "it was through the[sic] evangelical Protestantism that Platonized Christianity found its most comfortable home in America."[18] A clear-cut division of this worldly and otherworldly, the body and the soul, the individual and the society, were all specialties or features of this spirituality. Protestant emphasis on an otherworldly spirituality promoted an escapist mode of spiritual activities among black people, and also shaped their theological consciousness. To some extent, it worked as a reactionary response of blacks to the experience of slavery. Moreover, this type of Platonized Christian influence promoted closed monotheism and made absolute claims on spiritual purity and holiness. In effect, the Platonic dispositions in Protestant faith legitimized the attacks on blacks, which were sanctioned by the white cultural ideology.

Protestantism and Black Faith

Douglas notes another important element in Protestantism about black faith. As mentioned earlier, black people were attracted to the Protestant faith because it provided a new space for blacks to affirm themselves and their traditions. Many also attribute this attraction to their "innate" inclination towards emotion and passion. But Douglas says that black people were not passive recipients of Christian Protestantism; rather, they scrupulously appropriated it because it could conform to their own theological and cultural affirmations. In summation, black people adopted evangelical Protestant theology and appropriated the body-soul divide as a response to their problem. The response emerged as a protest against the sexual stereotyping of black bodies. The interesting point is

18. Douglas, *What's Faith Got to Do with It?* 133.

that the Protestant traditions served to help black people (especially black women) reclaim control over their bodies (agency) at the same time as its theological content continued to be Platonized. Douglas interestingly refers to the protest of black Protestant Puritans against Martin Luther King Jr's civil right movement, as they were busy with saving the individual black souls![19]

RELEVANCE OF DOUGLAS'S CRITIQUE IN DOING WOMANIST THEOLOGY

Douglas's theoretical critique is very relevant to womanist theology. The critique helps us reimagine the theological engagements of black people in light of new theoretical groundings. She reclaims a hermeneutical paradigm for black theological expressions. It is the "hermeneutic of appropriation" which has been the core of black faith tradition. The hermeneutic of appropriation tries to bridge the gap between the "spiritual" and "historical." Moreover, this hermeneutical principle affirms critical engagements with the Bible and shapes core theological themes based on equality, justice, and love. Douglas argues that this is in continuity with the African theological expressions and heritage. "Everything is sacred," and "secularity has no reality."[20] Such concepts are historically aligned with black expressions. By drawing theological resources from African theological expressions, Douglas tries to create new trajectories for black womanist theologies. Moreover, she reimagines womanist theology as a meaningful engagement for harmonious relationality. Douglas adds, "Womanist Theology would affirm the necessity for sexual expression to be relationally right; that is, an intimate expression of loving, harmonious relationality."[21] Thus, Douglas's theological and theoretical arguments compile an inside and outside critique of black reality, which is so relevant and important for black and womanist theologies today.

19. Douglas, *What's Faith Got to Do with It?*, 144.
20. Douglas, *What's Faith Got to Do with It?*, 157.
21. Ibid., 215.

The Problem of Platonized Black Faith

As previously discussed, Platonic black faith is problematic because of its dualistic world view. In this section, Platonized black faith is re-evaluated from a womanist perspective. This section tries to explain how the patriarchal force works in the black church and how it is problematic.

Patriarchal Discourse within Black Faith

The patriarchal dispositions of black faith placed black women into the category of second-class citizens. And, it's interesting how patriarchy and the discourse of power are intertwined within the black community. Douglas explains this by using James Baldwin's novel *Go Tell it on the Mountain*.[22] The relationships are controlled, domesticated, suppressed, broken, and abused by the dynamics of Platonized power and patriarchy. The more patriarchy exercises its power on women by sexualizing them, the more it establishes a broader unjust alliance of racism, platonized Christianity, and sexism; hence, the patriarchy is cyclical in nature and enables itself to continue. The black woman's body has therefore become "extraordinarily exposed to violent exploitation."[23]

Platonized Sexual Ethic / Hyper Proper Sexuality

The patriarchal culture promoted by Platonized Christian faith conferred a privilege to black men and disregarded black women. The interplay between Platonized Christianity and patriarchy made black women objects of temptation and sin, where we see the black woman's body as a site of violence. This "oversexualization"[24]

---

22. Douglas uses two famous novels of James Baldwin, 'Go Tell it on the Mountain' and 'Amen Corner' to delineate the complexity of Black Protestant Spirituality.

23. Douglas, *What's Faith Got to Do with It?*, 187.

24. The word here refers to the act of interpreting black body as lustful and then exploiting.

of the black woman resulted in the adoption of a "hyper-proper" sexuality by black people. The hyper-proper sexuality is defined as a hyper-commitment to so-called "holy living," in regards to sexual purity. It can be understood as a hyper-reactive response to the Platonized Black Faith and white cultural ideology. In effect, the patriarchy within the black church treated black women as sexualized and then victimized them.

Womanist Critique of Black Faith

Faith has been used as a tool by black people to navigate their experience of struggle. This faith has enabled blacks to sustain their life and dignity in a hostile experience, particularly in the social context of America. But according to Douglas, there are both positive and negative aspects of this black experience. Douglas points out that "Even as the black faith tradition was born out of and speaks to the black experience of struggle, it has been both a bane and blessing for black people."[25] Black faith has been a blessing because it created a sacred canopy of protection for black bodies, and it has been a bane because it offered "theological justification for the denigration of black bodies."[26] A womanist critique of black faith appreciates the liberating aspects of black Christian faith and tries to free it from its oppressive dispositions like patriarchal nature, dualistic tendencies, etc. A womanist critique of black faith encourages appreciation of the following elements of black faith.

Core Theological Themes

Black faith is distinct in its theological core, and according to Douglas the core theological themes of black faith should be appreciated and affirmed for a meaningful womanist theological engagement. These themes emerged from concrete black experiences, and Douglas identifies these core themes of black faith as

25. Douglas, *What's Faith Got to Do with It?*, 199.
26. Ibid.

positive contributions to womanist expressions. The "spirituality of resistance." The spirituality that helped people to live with dignity in the context of slavery, oppression and exploitation is merely a "spirituality of resistance."[27] It is shared and passed down through generations by black grandmothers and grandfathers. The tenacity of black people to survive against all the odds has come out of this spirituality. Harmony is another important theological theme of black faith, which has roots in African community life. The African tradition strives for harmonious relationality. The God/human/nature harmony is affirmed by African theological expressions. Such a harmonious relationality is one of the core affirmations of black faith. However, "slavery fundamentally denied any notions of harmony."[28]

Hermeneutic of Appropriation

For a meaningful womanist critique of black faith, that faith must be seen as a tool. Douglas proposes a new way of interpreting that faith: "Hermeneutic of Appropriation." The Hermeneutic of Appropriation concept is based on the historical black experience. The Christian faith of the oppressor was not blindly received by black people. Blacks appropriated it and made it relevant to their everyday experiences. Such an appropriation of black faith should be done through womanist engagements for an authentic method of interpretation. According to Douglas, a Hermeneutic of Appropriation "would prompt womanist discourse to go beyond racial constructs in its responses to the consistency of the black faith tradition."[29] Moreover, it could push womanist theology to take the issues of environment, disability, and sexuality more seriously.

---

27. Douglas, *The Black Christ*, 105.
28. Douglas, *What's Faith Got to Do with It?*, 201
29. Ibid., 209.

New Discourse on Sexuality

The Hermeneutics of Appropriation can help us re-orient our notions of sexuality. While the intimate relationality within the sex is rejected by Platonized Christianity, womanist interpretation is trying to retrieve this element. Within the heterosexual discourses on sexuality promoted by Platonized Christianity, there are only two possibilities: either "procreatively good or lustfully bad."[30] But here there is a third way: to emphasize sexuality regarding relationality and intimacy. This is the fundamental standpoint of womanist theology, fighting for justice, love, and harmony. Douglas says, "the womanist challenge today is to retrieve the connection between sexuality and loving relationships."[31] By interpreting sexuality beyond the Platonic dualism, womanist discourse fights for a new body politic based on relationality, mutuality, love, intimacy, justice, and harmony. Therefore there are multiple possibilities other than heterosexuality which are all celebrated.

New Trajectories for Womanist Theology

From these theological affirmations and critiques, we can imagine new trajectories for womanist theology. Womanist interpretation establishes "blackness"[32] as a liberation commitment, creating a liberating solidarity with the oppressed, like Dalit/tribal women. Such an experience of "walking together" can only make womanist theology more womanist. By interpreting sexuality in terms of relationality and harmony, womanist theology opens up new hermeneutic spaces for sexual minorities. The environmental crisis calls for a meaningful womanist liberating spirituality too. The disability debate should also be taken into serious consideration for an inclusive womanist theological engagement. So the new

---

30. Ibid., 214.
31. Ibid., 215.
32. Womanists affirm "Black is Beautiful." The argument is placed against the dominant white aesthetic construction. See Maxine Williams, "Black Women and Struggle for Liberation," para. 3.

trajectories of womanist theology in the twenty-first century will be multifaceted. Womanist Eva E. Carruthers says that one of the challenges of womanist theology is a crisis of memory. She names it as a culture of amnesia. "The culture of amnesia is the complete embodiment of collective forgetfulness. We now have the generations of persons in the pulpit and pew, churched and unchurched, who are clueless about how they got where they are, why they are there, where they are, and what they ought to be doing."[33] She reminds us of the *Sankofa* bird in West Africa, whose beak touches its tail as a reminder about the circle of life.[34] It is a call to look back to move forward. For an oppressed community, memory is a tool to fight against the ongoing injustice.

---

33. Hopkins and Thomas, *Walk Together Children*, 299.
34. Ibid., 300.

Chapter 5

The Problem of History and Taxonomy in Sanskritic Traditions

THE CONCEPTS OF HISTORY and taxonomy are critical in Sanskritic traditions of India. Without a serious consideration of them, we cannot have a meaningful critique of the epistemological foundations of Sanskritic traditions. The "eternality" of Vedas has been emphasized by the cost of "history." Thus, history is devalued. In the same way, the Vedic taxonomical accounts have established an epistemological basis for the corresponding hierarchical social module. I attempt here to critically analyze the notion of history and taxonomy in the Sanskritic traditions to explicate how they are epistemologically problematic.

Epistemology is like a tinted glass. When we look at things through stained glass, we get tinted images of things according to the corresponding color scheme in the glass. Just like this, the nature of perceiving and understanding things is very much grounded in epistemology. In this essay, I am trying to delineate two epistemological problems in the Sanskritic traditions of India. They are the problems of history and taxonomy. These themes are already pursued and examined by scholars like Sheldon Pollock and Bruce Lincoln.[1] In this article, I would like to explore how the problem of history is relevant to the issue of taxonomy in the Sanskritic traditions.

By epistemology, I mean the theory of knowledge. The term history refers to the historical events and facts and its progression within time and space. Since the term history is defined in terms of time and space, it is closely related to the social relations, which are being formed, reformed, and deformed within that time and space. The next category widely used in this article is taxonomy. Taxonomy represents a classificatory system, and the classification process is a demarcating process. It orders things based on corresponding scales. Taxonomy is an ordering system. By Sanskritic traditions, I mean the Brahmanical traditions in India which include Vedas and Upanishads.

HISTORY

The historical consciousness is ambiguous in Sanskritic traditions. There are scholars who consider history as a "zero category,"[2] and others who find historicity within the Sanskritic traditions. It is tough to locate the concept of history as a chronological and systematic narration of events in the Sanskritic traditions. But we can find some historical consciousness within the Sanskritic traditions itself. The concepts are demonstrated in Yuga, Karma, Itihasa, Puranas, etc.

However, a different level of argument can be posed to solve the problem based on Ricoeur's idea of the historicity of narrative. He says that "Narrative itself is the linguistic form of human temporal experience."[3] If narrative can be considered as something historical in itself (as Ricoeur suggests), Sanskritic traditions can

---

1. See Sheldon Pollock, "Mīmāṃsā and the Problem of History in Traditional India," 603–10, and Bruce Lincoln, *Discourse and the Construction of Society*, 131–41.

2. Larson, *Karma as 'a Sociology of Knowledge*, 305.

3. Quoted in, Pollock, *Mīmāṃsā and the Problem of History in Traditional India*, 604.

claim its historicity based on that. But there is a question regarding how the Sanskrit texts figure into this temporality as the Sanskritic traditions claim the transcendent nature of the texts. But one can feel a general absence of "historical referentiality" within the Sanskritic traditions. Pollock comments on this issue as something very arresting. An overall lack of historical referentiality in traditional Sanskritic culture remains a problematic, and possibly unparalleled, phenomenon.[4]

Despite many references to the historic consciousness in the Sanskritic traditions, history is still problematic because the Sanskritic traditions don't consider history as having an epistemological value and significance. The historicity of human existence was cognized (not exactly as an explicit theory and reflection), appropriated, and processed in traditional India, but differently. But the historical conscious became diminished because of something beyond history. Pollock writes: "The concrete events are perceived and recorded, while at the same time they are located in a parallel context—the divine—that offers an interpretation of their ultimate meaning."[5] Placing history below something eternal (beyond time and space), i.e. Vedic truth, was the way through which history received no interpretative value.

To analyze the problem of history, we need to have a deeper look at the Mimamsa School of Thought. The Mimamsa School of Indian Philosophy was considered to be the culturally normative discipline of Brahmanical learning. The Mimamsa theory of knowledge is based on the Vedic knowledge. Mimamsa claims of truth and authority had significant influence in attributing history a lower epistemological position. The presuppositions of the Mimamsa School of Thought have been determined to be one of the reasons for the "ahistoricality" element. According to Pollock, Mimamsa influenced Sanskritic discourses "to deny the category of history altogether as irrelevant, or even antithetical, to real knowledge."[6] The real knowledge is something that cannot be cog-

4. Ibid., 607.
5. Ibid., 606.
6. Ibid.

nized by any other knowledge. The following factors are at work for the "ahistoricality" in Sanskritic traditions:

1. The epistemological base of the Mimamsa School lies in the doctrine of Svatah Pramanya. This is the theory of intrinsic validity. Daniel Arnold comments on this aspect of Mimamsa epistemology like this: "characteristically, the Mimamsa claim is that this desideratum must be possessed or conferred intrinsically."[7] The claims of truth (here Vedas), as something intrinsically true are problematized here. There are various opinions regarding this point. It depends on how we interpret the word *pramanya*. Daniel Arnold points to the problem of reading Mimamsaka epistemology as a fundamentalistic exercise.[8]

2. The second important thing is the Mimamsaka concept of dharma. Dharma is considered to be "a transcendent entity and so is unknowable by any form of knowledge not itself transcendent."[9] Svatah dharma is a concept of Mimamsa which confers eternality to dharma.

3. The theory of language in the Mimasa Sutra is founded on the idea of eternality of the language. This is the same theory purported by the grammarian Pathanjali: *"Siddhe sabdarthasambandhe"* (Patañjali's *Vyakarana Mahabhashya*). His theory affirms the eternal relation between the word and its meaning. This transcendent character *(nityatva)* of language contributed much to the "ahistorical" element in the Sanskritic texts.

4. The vedicization process is another important factor that works behind the ahistoricality. The Vedas are considered to be eternal in *Mimamsa Sutra*. Pollock refers to a process of vedicization (linking and connecting to Vedas and their by suppressing the historicality). He further explains "Veda

---

7. Arnold, *Buddhists, Brahmins, and Belief*, 60.
8. Ibid.
9. Ibid.

as the general rubric under which every sort of partial knowledge—the various individual *sastras*—are ultimately subsumed."[10] By calling *Itihasa* the Fifth Veda, it is linked to the transcendent Vedic texts and its eternality. Therefore, the *Itihasas* were accommodated to the eternity and thus to the 'ahistoricality' of Vedas through vedicization.

Therefore, there are several factors to be considered to explore the problem of history in Sanskritic traditions. Considering all the factors above mentioned, it is evident that history has been subsumed by the eternality of Vedas and scripture. The historical consciousness is not omitted because of mere disinterest, but it has been denied for an important truth claim by Mimamsakas. But what are the implications? The denial of history as an epistemological tool proposes an unending social system over the social process. If everything is given and eternal, what is the role of the process? Additionally, this argument privileges the structure of the social order over the creative role of humans in history. It also naturalizes the asymmetric power relations of the present. In the process of naturalization (making something "natural", or "given" through interpretation), texts also have an important role.

We have been discussing the problem of history in Sanskritic traditions, and how it is an epistemological problem. I think the problem of history should be considered along with the issue of taxonomy at this point. To do that, we will focus on the taxonomical systems in the following section.

TAXONOMY

Taxonomical modules are classificatory in intention; for example, the classification of books in a library. The books are sorted, organized, and arranged according to the corresponding classificatory system used by the library. This classification system is based on some parameters or scale (let us call them taxonomizers). The arrangement of books and documents, numbering, and locations; all

10. Ibid., 609.

are dependent upon the parameters or scales used by the library classification system. There are many more examples like this. The body/soul classification in Platonism is another example for taxonomical module based on dualism.[11]

Another example is the family dining arrangement aptly taken by Bruce Lincon. He takes the subjective experience of dining with his family. It was according to the system prevalent during 1950s and 1960s in American families.[12] He notes that the special way of a customary positioning of the members of the family around the table during dining was not neutral, not value-free. He treats it as the taxonomical system. In the dining table, various taxonomizers were working, such as age and gender. The taxonomical ordering was based on these taxonomizers so that the older males were privileged. The same sort of taxonomies are found by Lincoln in various other cultural contexts.

All the taxonomies mentioned above are systems meant for classification. But they are epistemological more than classificatory. At this point, I would like to focus on the taxonomical account in the *Chandogya Upanishad* 6.1–6. The text is about a conversation between the wisdom teacher Uddalaka Aruni and his son Svetaketu.[13] The conversation progresses with the idea of three quasi-substantial entities by which the entire universe is constituted. They are 1) Tejas (radiant energy), 2) Apas (water), and 3) *Annam* (food).[14] The sequential order in which the primordial forms are created should be noted here

1. Tejas—(Radiant Energy)
2. Apas—(Water)
3. Annam—(Food)

This creation order is placed here as a primary threefold taxonomical module. Based on this module, other related modules can

---

11. Thilly, *A History of Philosophy*, 75.
12. Lincoln, *Discourse and the Construction of Society*, 131.
13. Olivelle, *The Early Upanishad*, 245.
14. *Chandogya Upanishad*, 6.2.3 and 6.2.4

be created; for example, the Origin of Creatures. The order would be creatures from eggs, living individuals, and sprouts (*ChU* 6.3.1). The corresponding sequential order of the first module is applied here. The origin of the color scheme described is also in the same order: red, white, and black (*ChU* 6.4.1). The body imagery exactly fits into the threefold module (*ChU* 6.5–6). The nine components of the body are categorized into three modules. They are (in sequential order),

1. Mind, Flesh, and Feces
2. Speech, Marrow, and Bones
3. Breath, Blood, and Urine

A hierarchical ranking in the order of creation can be noted in the text. The sequence is just like first, second, and third order. A vertical ranking is also explicit in these modules. If we put the module in the vertical position the things are arranged by a "scale of relative density."[15] According to Lincoln, this taxonomical categorization is done by two taxonomizers. They are "elevation" and "purity."[16] When it goes upwards in the taxonomical module, purity increases, whereas when it goes downward, purity decreases.

Such a ranking in the taxonomical module is not neutral. Lincoln infers a social module based on these basic modules. Even though there is no reference to the social category, it can be easily understood from these modules. By the two taxonomizers, elevation and purity, the two noble castes (priests and warriors) will form the upper strata, and the commoners form the lower strata.[17] When it goes upward in this module, purity increases, and things become finest. When it goes downward, the purity decreases. Then, naturally, it legitimizes the caste hierarchy. Lincoln shrewdly points out that "although *Chandogya* never advances a social module, one may not conclude that the text has no interest in social . . .

15. Lincoln, *Discourse and the Construction of Society*, 137.
16. Ibid., 138.
17. Ibid.,139&140.

by remaining implicit, which is to say masked, this hierarchic classification of social strata is placed beyond question."[18]

Lincoln emphasizes why the text is important and especially interesting: it is because the "society and social category are never mentioned in it."[19] Why is this? Since the category of social is never mentioned in the Vedic account, there is only a possibility to infer the social dimension of it, as Lincoln suggests. But here I would like to connect Pollock's arguments about the ahistoricality of Sanskritic traditions. The next section is an exploration of this issue.

CONNECTIONS

The Mimamsa tradition (particularly Purva Mimamsa) takes Vedic literature as the authoritative text. To emphasize the epistemological frame of Mimamsa tradition, Daniel Arnold specifically looks at the authoritative texts of Mimamsa. He writes: "the *Mimamsa Sutra* is the application of the Vedic literature in particular of the earlier part of that corpus, chiefly *Brahmana*s."[20] Since Brahmanas are the authoritative texts for Mimamsa, the eternality of Brahmanas is affirmed. Considering the case of *Chandogya Upanishad*, it is a part of the *Chandogya Brahmana*. Patrick Olivelle says "the *Chandogya* is a section of the *Chandogya Brahmana* that belongs to the Tandya School of the Samaveda."[21] Therefore the eternality of the *Chandogya Upanishad* is proposed by the Mimamsa tradition.

Another consideration about the eternality of the *Chandogya Brahamana* is its affinity towards speech and chanting. Signe Cohen puts it like this; "*ChU*, more than any other *Upanishadic*[sic] text, dwells on the mystical efficacy of spoken language."[22] Cohen refers the primary importance of speech or chant given by the *Chandogya Upanishad*. Chants and speech are considered as eter-

---

18. Olivelle, *The Early Upanishads*, 140.
19. Lincoln, *Discourse and the Construction of Society*, 137.
20. Arnold, *Buddhists, Brahmins, and Belief*, 59.
21. Olivelle, *Upanishads*, 95.
22. Cohen, *Text and Authority*, 108.

nal in the ritual context of *Chandogya*. Olivelle also emphasizes the role of the *Chandogya* in the Samavedic chant. The *Chandogya* chant is deemed to be the High Chant (*Udgitha*).[23] The selected text in the *Chandogya Upanishad* 6:1–6 to which the taxonomical account of primordial forms referred belongs to the High Chant, and so the eternality of language in the *Chandogya Upanishad* is proved. The the *Chandogya Upanishad* stands in line with the Vedas, which prefers the eternality of language, and thereby precision, in chanting.

Signe Cohen gives a better explanation of the *Chandogya Upanishad*'s connection with the idea of textual authority. Cohen intelligibly narrates the textual formation of the *Chandogya Upanishad* and its relation with Rigveda. He writes; "the composers of the *Chandogya Upanishad* are attempting to negotiate a space for their text and the textual tradition of the *Samaveda* vis-à-vis the textual authority of the *Rigvedic* tradition."[24] The *Chandogya Upanishad* composers fight for sharing "Vedic authority" of Rigveda. Cohen also points that the *Chandogya Upanishad* accepts and embraces "the authority of the *Rigveda* and, suggests that the *Samaveda* is inseparably linked to the *Rigveda*."[25] It is implied that the "authority of the *Rigveda* is reflected in its partner text, the *Samaveda*."[26] So it is well evident that the *Chandogya Upanishad* shares textual authority with the Vedas.

All the aspects mentioned above refer to the point that the *Chandogya Upanishad* is consistent with the Mimamsa epistemology. Since Mimamsa presupposes the eternality of Vedas and Vedic truth, the *Chandogya Upanishad* also does the same. It denies a "historical consciousness" and references because of the prominence given to the eternality of the text. When we analyze the *Chandogya Upanishad* in the light of Mimamsa theory, it is well evident that it cannot have a historical referentiality by accounting a social module. So, my conclusion is that the taxonomical account

23. Olivelle, *Upanishads*, 95.
24. Cohen, *Text and Authority*, 101.
25. Ibid.
26. Ibid.

in the *Chandogya* denies historical references and thereby a social module to emphasize the eternality of the primordial forms.

This will be clearer when we consider other textual references to social modules. There are explicit references to social modules in *Manu Smriti* (12.24–50), *Bhagavad Gita* (18.7–48), and *Vishnu Purana* (16). But it should be noted that these traditions are not consistent with Mimamsa traditions, and they are not considered authoritative. But in the case of the *Chandogya Upanishad* as a primary authoritative text for Mimamsa (as it is a part of the *Chandogya Brahmana*) the same problem of history continues. Since history is considered epistemologically worthless, the text is silent about any historical reference. This is the same reason for the lack of a corresponding social module, because social relations are historically formed.

The problem of history and the question of taxonomy in Sanskritic traditions are epistemological problems. History has been subsumed by the overemphasis of the eternality of the Vedas, proposed by Mimamsa tradition. At the same time, the taxonomical account in the *Chandogya Upanishad* orders things in a hierarchical pattern. Unlike other narratives, the *Chandogya Upanishad* is silent about a social module which has historical implications. It is evident that the omission of historical references and thereby social referentiality is because of the Mimamsa epistemological influence. As the Mimamsa epistemology rejects the historical, then the social is also denied.

Chapter 6

Kammatipaadam as Subaltern Sthala Purana
Dalit Spatial Discourses and Micro-Eschatology

"For those in the margins, time is an ally as long as they are in the eschata fighting for proper space."[1]

—Vitor Westhelle

"The sacred is the last thing—*eschaton* . . ."[2]

—Richard Kearney

THE VERY LAST SCENE of the popular Malayalam movie *Kammatipaadam*[3] still haunts me. In the scene, there is an image of a

1. Westhelle, *Eschatology and Space: The Lost Dimension in Theology Past and Present*, 121.
2. Kearney, *Reimagining the Sacred*, 33.
3. *Kammatipaadam* is an Indian movie in the Malayalam language released in May 2016. It is directed by Rajeev Ravi and written by P. Balachandran. The name *Kammatipaadam* is primarily a spatial reference to a "water-rich paddy field" gradually turned into a slum locality in Ernakulam City (also known as Cochin), Kerala. The movie narrates how the Dalit

Kammatipaadam as Subaltern Sthala Purana

liminal space, which is beautifully and intelligibly engraved. It is an image of a narrow road from the Dalit colony, Kammatipaadam, to the street, enclosed by long wooden fences on both sides. The dead body of a Dalit youth, fully wrapped in white cloth, is being taken to the funeral pyre through that narrow path by his relatives and close friends. I believe this scene represents Dalit plight and struggles in the Indian state of Kerala today. The Dalit social condition in contemporary Kerala is closely related to the micro-geopolitics of their context. I want to take the above-mentioned scene from the movie as a hermeneutical key to understand and theologize subaltern spatial discourses and struggles with an eschatological sensibility. This paper attempts to re-read the Malayalam movie *Kammatipaadam* with the subaltern[4] and critical spatial sensibilities to re-signify the relevance of Dalit struggles for land and resources. This paper also tries to explain the micro eschatological dimensions embedded within the spatial location of Dalits and in their struggles.

---

community was forced to give up their lands to real estate mafias, and how the process gentrification of Cochin Metro City took place over the plight of the Dalits. See "Kammatipaadam," https://en.Wikipedia.org/w/index.php?title=Kammatipaadam&oldid=748289100, and http://primamovie.com/tag/kammatipaadam-full-movie-englishsubtitles/.

4. The term "subaltern" is used in this article with a contextualized meaning, referring to the Dalits in India. Dalits are the "outcaste" according to the caste system. The term was popularized by the Italian Marxist, Antonio Gramsci, to denote non-elite or subordinated social groups. It gained importance in India after the work of a group of thinkers who are usually referred to as Subaltern Studies Collective. Between 1982 and 1996, the Subaltern Collective published nine volumes on South Asian history and society. In the preface to the first volume, *Subaltern Studies*, Ranajit Guha proposes "subaltern" as a generic term to refer to "the general attribute of subordination in South Asian societies irrespective of its expression regarding class, caste, age, gender, and office, or in any other way." (Ranajit Guha, Preface to *Subaltern Studies,* vii.) An extended critique of the notion of subaltern is advanced by Gayatri Chakravorty Spivak. See Spivak, "Subaltern Studies: Deconstructing Historiography," 330–363.

Rhizomatic Reflections

THE REPRESENTATIONAL HISTORY OF DALITS IN MALAYALAM SCREEN

Generally, in Malayalam movies, Dalits are misrepresented or invisible. The mainstream Malayalam films cater to the cultural ethos of the high caste. The image of Malayali woman and man is conceptually and aesthetically stereotyped into the image of the Nair[5] woman and man. The aesthetics employed in these movies primarily relate to the so-called higher caste ethos, which reinstitutes the image of the light-complexioned, skinny woman and the heroic, fair-skinned strong man. Such stereotyping has made very little room for the representation of Dalits as the leading role in the movies. As a result, Dalits are always misrepresented as thugs, prostitutes, uneducated, etc. When the heroine of the first Malayalam movie—*Vigathakumaran*—was a Dalit Christian woman named P. K. Rosy, it was not well received by the Kerala people. She has to flee to Tamilnadu because she was attacked by the high-caste Nair landlords. Jenny Rowena writes of this event: "On the very first day on which her [P. K. Rosy's] film was released, men from the upper caste Nair community tore the screen and broke up the show, unable to bear the sight of a Dalit woman in the role of a Nair woman acting out love scenes with another man."[6] Even now, Dalits are excluded not only from the cultural landscape, but also from the media-scape of Kerala.

As a popular media, the film industry has a critical role in disseminating and constructing discourses on social life and relations. As the media plays an important role in making cultural representations, the invisibility or misrepresentation of both Dalit body and Dalit life in the movies should be problematized and analyzed. Sujith Kumar Parayil comments that the problem of the misrepresentation of Dalit life in the movies is expressed in two ways. "The first one is a visible and direct representation of the

---

5. The name of a higher caste in India, who were the main stewards of the land property in Kerala at the time of the feudal system, now endowed with much socio, economic, political, and cultural capitals.

6. Rowena, "Locating P K Rosy," para. 1.

physiognomy of the character as subaltern."[7] This direct representation of Dalits often turns out on the screen as the stereotyped characters like house maids, drunkards, helpers, villains, etc. Parayil continues: "the second way is through the deployment of an indirect and sometimes, invisible social and cultural signifier [sic] which indicate the subaltern identity (sometimes as elite subaltern) of the character."[8] In both ways, Dalit bodies and lives are represented by consciously putting them on the "other side" of the customary. This conscious activity of "othering"[9] Dalit bodies and lives point to the issue of autonomy of representation. In the cultural landscape of Kerala, Dalits do not enjoy the economic, social, and cultural capital to exercise the autonomy of their cultural representation. A long struggle awaits the subaltern communities for them to exercise their autonomy to represent themselves in the public space of Kerala. This autonomy also includes the ability to resist becoming passive consumers of the negative stereotypes of our misrepresented selves on the silver screen, caricatured by the high caste filmmakers. I hope this transformation will occur through the assertive actions, through unpacking their perpetual struggle, resistance, heroism, suffering, and joys. Malayalam screen is simply a representation of this representational dilemma.

LOCATING *KAMMATIPAADAM*: REDIRECTING THE GAZE

Even though there are many problems in the cultural representation and body politic of Dalits in the movie, *Kammatipaadam* prompts a different gaze to the geopolitics in Kerala. This makes the movie special. The story tells about the transformation of Cochin/Ernakulam, from its green past of paddy fields to a metropolitan city replete with skyscrapers as a part of "gentrification."[10]

  7. Parayil, "Visual Perception and Cultural Memory," 67.
  8. Ibid.
  9. The conscious political activity of making "other" in social space.
  10. "Gentrification" is a process of renovation and revival of deteriorated urban neighborhoods using the influx of more affluent residents, which results

The water-rich agricultural land, which is owned by Dalits, is destroyed in the name of a "smart city." Eventually, the Dalits become displaced as a result. The growth and expansion of a city occurs at the expense of the lives of the poor Dalits. The story shows how a city, with its appetite for land, consumes the identity, culture, and living spaces of the marginalized people. Almost all the scenes in the movie swing between the realities of life and death. Madhu Neelakandan's frame flows with the theme of the story. The movie clearly tracks the changes happening to the landscape of Kammatipaadam; it gradually transforms from a wide green space into to a divided, fenced plot with many huge concrete buildings. Eventually, this dramatic transformation of the landscape ends with the displacement of the Dalit people, who were the original inhabitants of the land.

Kammatipaadam: The Plot

The story is told through the eyes of Krishnan, one of the heroes of the movie. Through his eyes, the audience sees the lives of the people in Kammatipaadam, the original inhabitants of the land. The movie starts with the title song, "Para para," as a background score to a beautiful scene of a water-rich paddy field. Then the camera zooms into the life of Krishnan, who works in a security firm in Mumbai. Krishnan travels back to Kerala to meet Ganga, his childhood friend, after receiving a call from him. The story progresses through the memory of Krishna in a non-linear manner. The friendship between Krishnan and Ganga has many inter-caste dimensions and body politic, as Krishnan belongs to a higher caste, and Ganga is a Dalit. This inter-caste dynamic also becomes visible in the love affair between Krishnan and Anitha, the heroine of the movie. Anitha, the female cousin of Ganga, is a stereotypical Dalit girl. Krishnan and Ganga are being introduced to violence through Baalan, their mentor and a gangster. The role of Surendran, a local businessman, is very important in the story.

in increased property values and the displacing of lower-income families and small businesses.

At the beginning of the story, Surendran (known as Ashaan—the master in the movie) is a small businessman, but eventually becomes an agent of a real-estate mafia and cheats the people in Kammatipaadam. Surendran deceitfully uses Baalan and his gang to work for his selfish ends. The gang continues to be a tool in the hands of the wicked master without realizing that they are creating many enemies. The gang destroys the homes of the locals, which leaves Ganga's grandfather devastated. The death of the grandfather haunts Baalan, causing him to end his violent lifestyle and settle down with a family. However, after Baalan is killed brutally by their enemy Johnny, Krishnan goes on to run a travel agency. Meanwhile, Ganga remains a thug. Eventually, Krishnan relocates to Mumbai after an arrest, and Ganga marries Anitha. Krishnan comes back from Mumbai after he learns about mishaps created by Ganga, and tries to save him. Krishnan is left heartbroken when he hears that Ganga's dead body has been found. He later realizes that Ganga was killed by the Master Surendran himself, who has become a prominent business entrepreneur. Krishnan then kills Surendran by kicking him out the window of his high-story apartment. In the aftermath, Krishnan says that it is people like Surendran who corrupt the city, spilling blood for more lands and profit, and that he acted for the sake of his hometown, Kammatipaadam. The story embodies the anger, rage, resentment of the people who became displaced from their land.

A Contested Mini-Narrative

The narration of the story can be seen as a "mini-narrative." Mini-narratives are always in contestation with "meta-narratives."[11] Meta-narratives are used to legitimant dominant knowledge and

---

11. Lyotard problematizes grand narratives, by which a culture tells itself about practices and beliefs, and rejects mini-narratives that explain small practices and local events. The postmodern theoretical turn argues for the incredulity of grand narratives and the importance of mini-narratives. See Lyotard and Jameson, *The Postmodern Condition: A Report on Knowledge*, xxiv–xxv.

validate particular institutions.[12] By narrating the story of a land through the complex story of Dalit people, the movie intersects many mini-narratives. The sequences in the movie are not strictly chronological and longitudinal. It is thick and latitudinal in its method—which includes digressions, flashbacks, and foreshadowing. The narrative dismantles all the meta-narratives about the Ernakulam/Cochin City as the beautiful, commercial, and international city in its ambiance. The narrative is also a mini-narrative of the "Dalit other" in the particular context of Kerala. *Kammatipaadam* thus rejects overarching meta-narratives about the story and of the land and people. It is not only a micro-narrative, but also a counter-discourse.[13] To the dominant discourses and narrations of history, land, and people. With its unique narrative and prolonged plot (over three hours), the viewers have trouble determining who the hero of the story is, and even what is going on! It is a very thick narrative with many layers. As this movie uses unique tactics in its storytelling, the movie introduces a counter discourse into the public space of Kerala.

Symbolic Reversals

The movie symbolically reverses the total aesthetic sensibility of the cultural landscape of Kerala. The movie celebrates the presence and visibility of dark/subaltern bodies. The black bodies of Vinayagan, Manikandan, and Anitha dismantles the stereotypes of the hero and the heroine in Malayalam cinema. But at the same time, the movie superimposes some features to the Dalit characters. The characters of Baalan and Ganga are characterized by their crooked yellow teeth. Ajit Kumar criticizes such imageries in the movie by saying: "The superimposing of such features to Dalit body is a type of ethnographic violence."[14] This points to the

12. Ibid., xxiv.

13. Discourse is a system which structures the way that we perceive reality. Counter-discourses are those that oppose the dominant and customary. Mills, *Michel Foucault*, 55.

14. Ajitkumar, *Kammatipaadam an Ethnographic Violence*.

limitation of the movie. Even though it celebrates the visibility of Dalit bodies and subverts the dominant aesthetic sensibility, the movie over-romanticizes the Dalit body. This act of romanticizing only helps to keep the Dalit body as the "other" and a "museum piece" in the cultural landscape of Kerala. Another remarkable reversal in the movie occurs through the images of domestic space. The customary Brahminical/elitist terms of *tharavaadu, kizhakini, govani, muttam, koalayi*, (distinct domestic spaces in Brahminical homes), etc., are replaced by Dalit domestic sensibilities. The traditional imageries of spacious homes and front yards are replaced by tiny, temporary, fenced domestic spaces and yards. The more "democratic" use of shared domestic space of Dalit homes is illustrated by the free physical movements of women characters like Rosamma, Anitha, and the mother of Ganga in their homes. Such symbolic reversals occur tactfully in the movie.

STHALA PURANAS AND THE PROBLEM OF DOMINANT CARTOGRAPHIES

Sthala puranas are very common in the Indian religious/cultural landscape. "Sthala" means space or land. "Purana" means story or narrative. Sthala purana can be translated as "land tale." There are many land narratives that are popular in India. These land narratives are not neutral in its motifs. All of these narratives cater to the land owners, the high-caste Hindus. Usually, these land narratives are related to Hindu divinities to legitimate the ownership of the land. It is challenging to demystify the dominant Hindu Sthala puranas and cartographies because they are invariably intertwined with the religious power, ritual practices, and knowledge system. Counter-narratives are much rarer in the cultural history of India.

Myths and Land Ownership

According to the popular myth, Kerala was reclaimed from the sea by Parasurama, an incarnation of Lord Vishnu, who gave it as a gift to the Brahmin settlers whom he had brought from outside the state. These Brahmin settlers enjoyed the "Janmom" rights (the absolute proprietorship on land). Gradually the land came to be handed over to sub-castes like Naduvazhis (Chieftains), Nairs, and others, creating various tenure rights. M. A. Oommen rightly observes that "At the lowest rung of the caste hierarchy as well as the landed hierarchy were the agricultural laborers."[15] The lower strata of the hierarchy cannot be even named as the laborers, but they were the slave castes, the Dalits who became displaced from the social system and also lacked the right to own the land. Sanal Mohan prefers to name this social condition of Dalits in the traditional society as "slavery," as the term meaningfully refers to the dynamics of hegemony and social control as a social construction.[16] Therefore, according to the myth of Parasurama, the original owners of the land in Kerala were the Brahmins and their control over the land was "divinely sanctioned." This myth consciously creates a hegemonic Brahminic cartography in Kerala. But this is contested by many scholars. The historian Elamkulam Kunjan Pillai has shed more light on the history of land ownership in Kerala. He observes that the Janmi-Kudiyan (master-steward-slave) system was a social hierarchy, consciously constructed after the migration/invasion of Aryans during seventh and eighth centuries in Kerala. "There is no evidence of a land-owning Brahmin class, during the *Sanghom* period (which ends by six hundred CE). And, on the contrary, there are pieces of evidence to show that land belonged to the so-called lower castes or scheduled castes today."[17] Thus, there is widespread consensus that the issue of land ownership is historically contingent and not divinely sanctioned.

15. Oommen, *Land Reforms and Socio-Economic Change*, 11.
16. Mohan, *Modernity of Slavery*, 39,
17. Pillai, *Jenmi Systems in Kerala*, 10.

Land Reform and Geopolitics in Kerala

Land reform was a helpful initiative to solve the issue of land distribution in Kerala. During the 1950s, there were several efforts to uproot the *Janmi-kudiyan* land-tenure system and to implement equitable distribution of land. One of the key legislations the state had undertaken to ensure that there was land for the landless was the Kerala Land Reforms Act, implemented in 1970. By this Act, the centuries-old Janmi-Kudiyan system was brought to an end. The Act was introduced with some amendments meant to establish a ceiling on land holdings. However, this act exempted both plantations and private forests. The Act also gave proprietary rights to cultivating tenants and protected the Kudikidappukars (cultivating tenants) from eviction. This piece of legislation was considered by many to be a revolutionary movement for the landless people. However, the proper implementation of the Act is another story. According to the Act, the government was to distribute surplus and revenue forest land to Kerala's landless poor. To date, however, the Act has not been fully implemented, which has caused a significant number of people in the state to become landless. P. T. George writes, "Although the Adivasis [tribal people] and Dalits form the backbone of the agricultural economy of Kerala, they have not yet benefitted from the land reforms that the Kerala Government initiated in the 1950s."[18] Various land distribution schemes and programs that were meant to minimize landlessness among the *Adivasis* and the Dalits failed to achieve that purpose. As far as the landlessness in Kerala is concerned, the Dalits and the Adivasis form around 85 percent of the landless in the state.

Kammatipaadam as Subaltern Sthala Purana

The very name itself, *Kammatipaadam*, is a spatial reference. Ernakulam/Cochin was a small township during the 1950s. The communist government allotted small tracts of farmland to the landless Dalit community. But after the economic liberalization of

18. George, "The Promised Land," 19.

1991, Kochi has transformed into a metropolitan city. The government started and implemented the Cochin Developmental Authority, which supported the real-estate boom. The very first shot of the movie is an eagle-eye view of Kammatipadam. It is a topological view of fertile land and the people who are living in close harmony with nature. The fertile land is rich in water. The film begins with a story of resistance from the perspective of the Dalits who are protesting against the claim of an outsider. The outsider claims that the land is under his ownership and they are not allowed to fish there. But the story progresses through the narration of the shrinking landscape through so many invasions and hegemony. Ashaan, who worked as a pimp to the real-estate companies, is a very important character in the movie. He uses Dalit youths to work as thugs for his gain. Gradually the fertile landscape becomes demarcated with many borders, walls, and fences.

Poetics/Politics of Space

There are references to the geographical location of Kammatipaadam throughout the narrative. Also, the domestic space of the Dalit colony is well-pictured and well-narrated. I believe that the movie initiates a spatial turn in Malayalam movie history, particularly from a subaltern point of view. This spatial turn assuredly demands a foil in the quotidian reading of the *eschata*[19] from a theological perspective. This is because the people of Kammatipaadam are already at the *eschata*. For them, *eschata* is quotidian.

This spatial dimension of everyday life can be rephrased as "poetics of space," as suggested by Gaston Bachelard.[20] Bachelard says that: "Not only our memories but the things we have forgotten

---

19. "Eschata" is a Greek word meaning "last things" or describing things as "last." The term thus has connotations to issues connected to the "last days," or "end of times." In the New Testament, "eschata" is used not only in a temporal sense but also in spatial sense, denoting the geographical ends or borders (Acts 1:8).

20. Bachelard and Stilgoe, *The Poetics of Space*, xxxvii.

are 'housed.'"²¹ He continues, saying that "Our soul is an abode. And, by remembering 'houses' and 'rooms,' we learn to abide within ourselves. Now everything becomes clear; the house images move in both directions: they are in us as much as we are in them."²² Kearney identifies this type of eschatological experience as "micro-eschatology." The movie, then, through the narration of Dalit lives in *Kammatipaadam*, challenges viewers to return to the *eschata*, here and now. "Such a return would invite us to experience the ultimate in the mundane."²³

Voicing Dalit Spatial Discourses

The narrative embodies Dalit spatial discourses in Kerala. Rajiv Ravi, the director of the movie, says that he used "realism" as a method to narrate the real lives of Dalits in Kerala who are struggling for land and resources.²⁴ Jayan Cherian, the director of another Dalit movie titled *Papilio Buddha*, said that these new trends in the Malayalam movie are an outcome of a butterfly effect of recent struggles of Dalit people for land in different spaces, namely in Chengara, Meppadi, and Muthanga.²⁵ These movies make a conscious effort to represent the Dalit lives in the popular media, where they have historically been misrepresented or invisible. Making visible and verbalizing Dalit spatial discourse in the popular media surely has so many repercussions.

21. Quoted in, Bahloul, *The Architecture of Memory*, vi.
22. Ibid.
23. Kearney, *Epiphanies of the Everyday*, 3.
24. Quoted by Nagarajan, "How Green was My City," 2.
25. Trivedi, *The Butterfly Effect*, para. 3.

Eschatological Implications of *Kammatipaadam*

Can these Fences Speak?

Throughout the spatial narration of the story of *Kammatipaadam*, from the beginning to the end, the geographical transitions of the territory are frightening. Even though the movie begins with a beautiful scene of fertile land in Kammatipaadam, it has become closed, divided, and wounded with many fences in only two years' time (from the conversation between Ganga and Krishna). The land has been sold to real-estate companies who are building new skyscrapers for the sake of constructing a "smart city."

Towards the end of the movie, the fences increase in number and Kammatipadam has shrunken in the spatial sense, leaving many people to be displaced. The death of Ganga becomes an emotional blow to both his father and to Krishnan. The dead body of Ganga is being taken through a very liminal passage, from his home to the public funeral pyre. Symbolically, that liminal space becomes a choratic space[26] where the people encounter life and death on an everyday basis. The large fences on both sides of the passage remain a representation of the mark of the wounded psyche of the Dalit people. "How [has] that passage become so narrow? Who made it?"[27] asks Vinayakan, the Dalit actor who played the character of Ganga.

Dalit Colonies as Choratic Spaces

The Dalit colonies in Kerala are the best examples of social segregation of Dalits.[28] In the context of particular geopolitics in Kerala, which has always had the caste system as a backdrop, the Dalits have become either colony dwellers or displaced ones. Colonies

---

26. Originally from the Greek word "Χώρα", *chora* has many dimensions of meaning. The most prominent and relevant one is "the space lying between two places or limits."
27. Malayalienter, "Kammatti Paadam Movie Review."
28. Trivedi, "The Butterfly Effect," para. 3.

Kammatipaadam as Subaltern Sthala Purana

are usually considered as the Dalit ghetto, a place of thugs and violence. The colonies are inside in and outside the society at the same time. They are at the margins. Margins always challenge the dominant social space. Y. T. Vinayaraj comments that "Marginality signifies a contingent social location which is neither inside nor outside of the system; rather it locates itself in the 'in-between' space."[29] This "in-between space" can be named as a *choratic* space. Margins, borders, fringes, and edges are liminal spaces (i.e., eschata) that demand serious theological reflection and analysis. Westhelle writes, "Eschatology is a discourse on liminality, marginality, on that which is in [an] ontological, ethical, and also epistemological sense different."[30]

Quotidian Eschata and Micro-Eschatology

Kammatipaadam poses many micro-eschatological challenges to us. According to Kearney, micro-eschatology is "the renewed attention to everyday epiphanies, which challenges us to encounter the 'other' in the relational infinity of our daily experience."[31] From a micro-eschatological sensibility, the actor Vinayakan, a native of the actual Kammatipaadam, cautions the Dalit people not to be fooled in the hands of masters.[32] This is a call for a repositioning. The very repositioning of the subjectivity can be a powerful social critique. According to Sunny Kapikkadu, a Dalit activist and philosopher, Dalit resistance should take the form of "assertive actions" to reclaim their ownership of the land.[33] These assertive actions are micro-eschatological in nature.

The *Kurichi* Strike, which occurred in 2000 February, is an example of a Dalit micro-eschatological event. The issue behind the strike was the charging of an eleven Kilo Volt electric line through the *Kurichi-Sachivothama puram* Dalit colony, without

29. Vinayaraj, *Ecclesiology with(out) Margins*, 86.
30. Westhelle, *Eschatology and Space*, 73.
31. Manoussakis, *After God*, xx.
32. Malayalienter, "Kammatti Paadam Movie Review."
33. Kapikkad, *Thiraskritharude Charisthram: Bhashanavum Yukthiyum*, 8.

any consensus with the colony dwellers. The electric line was a threat to the very life of the colony dwellers. The electric supply was a 'need' of a private factory owner. The colony dwellers protected against this. The protest of the people led to the suicide of Mr. Sreedharan.

The protest eventually strengthened with the solidarity of other secular participations. The Dalit people came together and asserted their right to live through a demonstration on February 27. Their slogan was assertive, "If the government is not withdrawing this 11 KV line, we will do it." And they did it. It was a micro-eschatological event that happened in the liminal space of the Dalits living in the caste-ridden civil society of Kerala. Such events reconstruct our society. It also dismantles the dominant knowledge-power system which relegates the Dalit people to the margins.

Dalit Cosmic Vision

Returning to the movie, the celebrated song "aa kanum mamalayonnum" embodies the Dalit cosmic vision. Ganga, the leading character in the movie, sings a song with an enchanting folklorist tune and taste. There is a moving sense of irony in the scene, as it is sung by a displaced Dalit. The song envisions a beautiful vision of harmonious living. The lyrics can be translated as: "Those mountains do not belong to us, these waters and its depth, and the river bank do not belong to anybody. Worm, tigers, birds, eagles, whales, and other animals, through the ages we coexist with the heavenly beings . . . we are living in such a planetary world." Of course, this is a Dalit utopian idea. Gail Omvedt emphasizes the relevance of such utopian Dalit visions.[34] Ravidas, a Dalit mystic lived in the fifteenth century, proposed a similar vision about a new city (not a village!) called "Begumpura." "Begumpura" depicts "a city without sorrow, with no taxes or toil, no exploitation, no

---

34. Omvedt, *Seeking Begumpura*, 268.

hierarchy, and freedom for all to walk anywhere."[35] Such a vision of a city beyond barriers is thoroughly Biblical and eschatological. It echoes the words of John of Patmos; "I saw the Holy City, the new Jerusalem, coming down out of heaven from God, prepared as a bride beautifully dressed for her husband" (Rev 21:2).

Kammatipaadam is not beyond criticism. But the spatial sensibilities of the movie generate a serious conversation about the role of caste in the geopolitics of Kerala. As a subaltern sthala purana, the movie demystifies, destabilizes, and dismantles the dominant sthala puranas like the Parasurama myth and its spatial politics. Such de-mythologization is apocalyptic and eschatological in its potentiality. The movie challenges us to realize the micro-eschatological moments embedded in the Dalit struggle for land and resources. The gradual progression of the land imagery, from a wide agricultural land to the narrow fenced path in the very last scene of the movie, still haunts me. In that *choratic* space, we meet the life and death of the Dalit people in *Kammatipaadam*. Yes, the fences can speak meaningfully and eschatologically.

35. Ibid.

Chapter 7

Re-Reading Ritual
Post-Enlightenment Theory and Subaltern Theology

"They [also] had a sense of the power of their rituals to transform their own lives. Thus, they created a counterhegemonic force through the use of rituals."[1]

—Linda E. Thomas

"Postmodernism provides epistemic space for the so-called 'theologies with pre-fix,' 'hyphenated theologies' and contextual theologies."[2]

—Y. T. Vinayaraj

THE OBJECTIVE OF THIS essay is to re-read the ritual from a subaltern perspective grounded in Post-Enlightenment theory[3] and

---

1. Thomas, *Under the Canopy*, 122.
2. Vinayaraj, "Envisioning a Postmodern Method of Doing Dalit Theology," 94.
3. The terminologies "Post-Enlightenment theory" and "postmodern theory" have been used interchangeably to refer to a theoretical break from

RE-READING RITUAL

to delineate the theological relevance of ritual practices for a meaningful subaltern Christian theological engagement in India. Obviously, the very first inquiry that can pop up is why a "re-reading"? A re-reading is necessary because the enlightenment hermeneutical sensibilities overlooked the formative role of ritual and valued belief over ritual, which is indicative of the notion of mind-body dualism.[4] This reductionist tendency is still prevalent in the Christian theological academia of India. I find that it is a serious theological neglect for Subaltern theology and there is a crucial need for a way out. This is the fundamental imperative of this re-reading experiment.

Why use the Post-Enlightenment hermeneutical theory as a grounding? It is because the epistemological shift initiated by Post-Enlightenment theory provides a new perspective to look into subaltern ritual traditions and symbolic worlds. And it challenges us to pick new hermeneutical possibilities and imaginations. This paper tries to glean these opportunities of Post-Enlightenment theory to develop a subaltern ritual hermeneutics so that it can help subaltern Christian theological engagements in India.

RE-READING RITUAL: CRITICAL ORIENTATIONS

The systematic historical and comparative cultural analysis of ritual has offered new insights into the dynamics of religion, culture, and society. There have been three significant developments in the modern study of ritual and myths. The first was the realization, associated especially with E. B. Tylor, J. G. Frazer, and

---

eighteenth-century European Enlightenment. The Post-Enlightenment theoretical (hermeneutical) turn indicates an inevitable departure from the contour of our orientation based on the knowledge system and the structures of enlightenment/modernity. Modernity is based on Cartesian dualism whereas the Post-Enlightenment research in ritual studies criticize this dualism and emphasize the embodied nature of ritual. Catherine Bell's work in this regard is central. See Bell, *Ritual Theory*, 76; Bell, *Ritual: Perspectives and Dimensions*, 3–60; Zuesse, *Ritual Cosmos*, 7; and Lincoln, *Discourse and the Construction of Society*, 137.

4. Bell, *Ritual Theory, Ritual Practice*, 95.

Emile Durkheim that the rituals of the primitive societies are closely related to the origin of religion. Ritual was considered the primitive way of reasoning. Durkheim tried to give a sociological interpretation of religion and ritual. The second was Sigmund Freud's discovery of the unconscious and its relation to myths and rituals. He considered ritual as neurotic compulsions. The third is the structural theory of myth and rituals propounded by the great French anthropologist Claude Levi-Strauss, who proposed an analysis of cognitive organization in cultural creations. The structural theory used a method of exploring a certain type of meaning through the binary opposition on which the anthropologists like Victor Turner, Edmund Leach, and Mary Douglas developed the ritual studies further. Catherine Bell groups these major schools in ritual studies into three loosely-knit families: 1) the myth and ritual school, 2) functionalists, neo-functionalists, and structuralists; and 3) culturalists, symbolists, and performance and practice theorists.[5] Mapping of a major theoretical shift is attempted in the next section with a particular emphasis on Post-Enlightenment hermeneutical turn in ritual studies.

THEORETICAL CONSIDERATIONS

The Enlightenment Sensibilities

The eighteenth-century European intellectual movement is known as the Enlightenment and defined by historians as a project of modernity. Regarding the understanding of the body, modernity constructed a philosophy of mind-body dualism in continuation with Platonic dualism. Paulose Mar Gregorios in his popular work entitled *A Light Too Bright* criticizes the project of modernity. He says that:

> The modern notion of separative self-desacralized nature has resulted in the marginalization of the people

---

5. Bell, *Ritual: Perspectives and Dimensions*, 3–60.

who lived in a symbiotic relationship with nature and rejected their knowledge as irrational and unscientific.[6]

The great pitfall of enlightenment theory is the concept of this "separative" self and the quest for universally valid meta-narratives. Naturally, it resulted in a rationalistic reductionism and overlooked micro narratives and little traditions.

The Epistemological Problem of Enlightenment

For Descartes, the prominent proponent of Enlightenment rationality, the reason-endowed subject was autonomous. For him, the rational human self is the "ultimate authority and center of reality."[7] The famous dictum "I think therefore I am" is a visible expression of the idea that the mind is an independent thinking substance. The mind is a metaphysical entity (disconnected with the body) which has its own potential to critically analyze everything. Immanuel Kant followed Descartes and proposed that there are a priori categories in mind and that they are universal.[8] It is also believed that the mysteries of the natural world can be resolved through scientific (objective, rational) means. The enlightenment hermeneutical paradigm envisaged a reason-endowed autonomous subject. Thus it presupposed that bodily activities are secondary, while mental thoughts are primary. This also resulted in a dualistic epistemology based on the mind-body divide. According to Catherine Bell, this enlightenment construction of dichotomy/binary opposites is a "process of homologization pushing for a loose systematization of several levels of homologized dichotomies."[9] Here it is worth noting Kelly Brown Douglas's observation on the influence of Enlightenment hermeneutical paradigm in the social construction of black body as subordinate. She says that "in many respects, owing to the

---

6. Mar Gregorios, *A Light Too Bright*, 29.
7. Jensen, *Theological Hermeneutics*, 79.
8. Kant, *Critique of Pure Reason*, 68.
9. Bell, *Ritual Theory, Ritual Practice*, 21.

spirit of the enlightenment, science fueled and kept alive the vital ideology necessary for white exploitative abuse of the black body."[10]

Disembodiment

The Enlightenment rationality presupposes a disembodied subject.[11] Thus the assumption has been that bodily movements are secondary and therefore whatever is going on in the movements of rituals must be something other than thinking. Rituals are consequently interpreted as non-cognitive behavior. This notion of dualism and disembodied objectivity is problematic because it is not a neutral territory. Whenever we have recourse to dichotomous thinking, there is always subordination.[12] There is a domination of mind over the body in the modernist epistemology. This is evident in the functionalist interpretation of rituals. In the functionalist interpretations, the ritual is often interpreted as a mechanical activity. In this case, the ritual actions are treated as merely a vehicle for thought, like an illiterate person carrying a book.

The Post-Enlightenment Sensibilities

The Post-Enlightenment theory is a break from the Enlightenment paradigm of disembodiment. By Post-Enlightenment theory I assume a broad spectrum of multidisciplinary theoretical resources, in the twentieth century, which go beyond Cartesian dilemma of binaries and disembodiment. The Post-Enlightenment theory is being used here as a tool at least in two different levels of its application. Firstly, in a general sense of drawing insights from the postmodern/Post-Enlightenment trends in anthropology, sociology, phenomenology, and linguistics.[13] Secondly, in a particular

10. Douglas, *What's Faith Got to Do with It?*, 119.

11. Disembodiment means placing human subject above the influence of the world, unaffected by it. Embodiment means to be influenced, affected and conditioned by history. Christopher Falzon, *Foucault and Social Dialogue*, 26.

12. Bell, *Ritual Perspectives and Dimensions*, 60.

13. For example the researches the anthropological studies of Victor

sense, it is more grounded in the recent anthropological researches on ritual by Catherine Bell, Ronald L. Grimes, Nick Crossley, Kevin Schilbrack, Evan M. Zuesse, and so on.

The Epistemological Shift

The critical shift that made by Post-Enlightenment theoretical turn was epistemological. It rejected modernist notion of disembodied self. It emphasized the social construction of self. Self is not a disembodied spectator; rather, it is "a construct of the social process through institutions, discourse, and practices."[14] The objects of thought are not naturally given. But they are the products of signs, symbols, and texts of the linguistic world. So thoughts are not a priori, but the endowed product of linguistic horizon and institutional practice. Hence human thoughts, emotions, bodily imaginations, social relations; everything is discursively constructed. Even the body is also embodied in the practices of the social world. Since the self, body, and social body are discursively constructed, it can be reconstructed. This possibility of reconstruction is an important theoretical emphasis in postmodernism. Another important shift was the rejection of the universalized notions of knowledge and affirmation of micro/local/little narratives. Michel Foucault calls such micro-narratives "subjugated knowledge."[15] The insurrection of such subjugated knowledges is resistive in nature. Here comes the relevance of subaltern religious/symbolic/ ritual life, which is resistive and constructive in a subtle and profound manner. Some of the Post –Enlightenment sensibilities on ritual are highlighted below, so that it may help us to go further in this research.

Turner, discursive approach of Michel Foucault, Post-Heideggerian phenomenology, and Wittgenstein in linguistic philosophy.

14. George, "Study," 14.
15. Foucault, *The Archaeology of Knowledge*, 3.

Ritual as Body Technique

The body is evidently more important in ritual. It engages our bodies and gives them a dignity on an immediate level. In a way, we can speak of the "Prestige of the Body" in ritual. These are conscious acts, lifted out of the general stream of actions and directed to transcendent ends. According to Nick Crossley, a postmodern social theorist, rituals are the "body techniques."[16] "Body techniques are culturally specific uses of the body."[17] They are the way in which, from society to society, people know how to use their body. They are the way of being in the world (*Dasein*, the Heideggerian concept[18]), rendering it intelligible and constituting it as a meaningful action. As ritual as body technique, it constitutes an integral part of being and becoming of the communities. The bodily involvement in the ritual dance of the tribal communities is the part of the celebration of the togetherness of the community. The *Chakka Bhajan*,[19] a ritual dance form of the Andhra Christians, is an active symbol of body technique.

Ritual as Ordering and Re-Ordering of Life

Nick Crossley also suggests that ritual is a "Call to Order."[20] To initiate a ritual is to make a compelling normative appeal to very deeply-rooted cultural dispositions. Others within the ritual community ought to respond and ought to experience the social pressure of this acutely (e.g., remaining seated during a national anthem requires considerable restraint. One's natural inclination

---

16. Crossley, "Body Technique," 33.

17. Ibid., 33.

18. The Heideggerian concept of "*Dasein*" (being-there) is all about the embodied nature of existence. This idea challenges the mind-body dualism of Enlightenment thought. See Heidegger, *Being and Time*, 57.

19. *Chakka Bhajan* is a ritual dance (*holding a special wooden piece in the hands of each performer*) of Andhra Christians (especially in the Rayalaseema area) which is performed on auspicious occasions. We can see a great bodily involvement and community celebration in this ritual dance.

20. Crossley, "Body Technique," 31.

is to rise). To initiate a ritual is to tap into these dispositions and, thereby to attempt to steer and channel the conduct of others.[21] It is precise to call them to order. There is a symbolic order behind every ritual. Through the ritual performance, this symbolic world is being disseminated. The symbolic order of ritual always challenges to order and re-order the social order.

Ritual as Punctuation of Life

In and through ritual a punctuation of time takes place. Life doesn't have meaning without punctuation of time, just like without punctuation there is no meaning of a sentence. Yearly festivals mark the moments in the life of the year, from birth through fertility to death. Even the minor moments of ritual, ignored by participants, render architecture in time in which the girders are ceremonial gestures, the rhythms of chant, the turn, and the chant. In the communities like Zen monasteries, Sufi orders, or Jewish mystical communities, the ritual often expands to fill every moment of daily life. The rhythm created by drumming, the stamping feet, etc., in various ritual practices are the means to keep "together" in time. Thus, "ritual" challenges us to punctuate our lives by marking a specific time through which we are given a temporal shape and meaning.

Ritual as Discourse

Grounded on the embodiment paradigm, ritual can be reimagined as a discourse. According to Michel Foucault, discourse is "the ways of constituting knowledges, together with the social practices, forms of subjectivity and power relations."[22] Such discourses of culture make sense of and give meaning to life. They structure consciousness and form communities. Mainly, they can serve members of subordinate classes in their attempts to

21. Ibid.
22. Foucault, *The Archaeology of Knowledge*, 3.

"demystify, delegitimize, and deconstruct the established norms, institutions, and discourses that play a role in constructing their subordination."[23] Thus the conception of ritual as discourse raises serious discussions about the micro-dynamics of symbolic power and social order. The underlying assumption of the discourse approach is that discourses have an important formative role in the construction, de-construction, and re-construction of human subjectivities.

Ritual as Practice

Catherine Bell defines ritual as *practice*.[24] The term practice means a form of embodied or practiced thought. It avoids the tendency to see ritual as expressive, irrational, merely emotional or cathartic. It goes beyond the functionalism. Bell argues for an analysis of ritual in the particular context. It maintains the synthetic unity of consciousness and social being within human activity. The important point regarding practice is that the social order, particularly the power relations, reproduce themselves in practices. The social order is maintained by institutions, discourses, and practices. So, it is quite evident that practices can change the social order. Hence, the ritual practices have a significant role in social change.

Undoubtedly, these Post-Enlightenment sensibilities on ritual provide a new perspective to re-look at subaltern ritual practices with a renewed spirit.

SUBALTERN THEOLOGY AFTER POST-ENLIGHTENMENT RITUAL STUDIES

Traditional Indian Christian Theology (ICT) kept a deaf ear to the subaltern religious symbolic world. ICT has been appropriating the Christian message to Hindu philosophy and culture.

---

23. Lincoln, *Discourse and the Construction of Society*, 5.

24. Bell takes the idea of practice from Pierre Bourdieu's concept of social practice and improvises it. See Bell, *Ritual Theory, Ritual Practice*, 76.

Sathianathan Clarke strongly criticizes this tendency as a hegemonic attempt to "baptize the gospel of Christ into the holy waters of Hindu Philosophy and Culture."[25] It didn't consider the culture and religion of the subaltern, who constitutes a significant portion of the Indian Christians. After the development of contextual and subaltern theological expressions like Dalit theology and Tribal theology in the 1980s, then the "subaltern identity" got much importance in the Indian theological arena. But we can still see a disconnect between subaltern Christian theology and subaltern religious sensibilities. Especially, in the area of subaltern ritual studies, seldom have academic works been done from a Christian theological perspective. This is a serious theological dismissal. To solve the issue, there should be conscious attempts to interconnect subaltern religion and theology. Subaltern ritual hermeneutics can contribute much to this effort. Since a detailed study is beyond the scope of this article, few insights are given below with the hope of further development.

Theologizing Subaltern Ritual Body

The Post-Enlightenment readings on subaltern ritual practices trigger new imaginations of the body. By consciously rejecting the imprints of the subordination, it challenges to re-signify the subaltern body as a potential agent to reorder the social body. This theoretical shift demands a theology of the subaltern ritual body.

Body as a Hermeneutical Key

For an authentic subaltern theologizing in India, the subaltern body should be considered as a hermeneutical key and a theological method. The "subaltern body" has been considered as impure, ambiguous, dangerous, and marginal in the caste society. But its potentialities like liminality, non-conformity, and orality reaffirm its messianic nature. A theological resignification of the subaltern

25. Clarke, *Dalits and Christianity*, 7.

ritual body emphasizes its potentiality to reimagine the social body. The symbolic inversion of the social positions in the ritual process is a great example for this. It is the celebrative exercise of the tortured body, and experiencing the resurrected body. The subaltern ritual body can be reimagined as Jesus's crucified body. For a Christian, the wounded body is the resurrected body, and the resurrected body is the wounded body. The subaltern ritual body is not a symbol of hopelessness, but it is the embodiment of hope.

"Ritualization" as a Hermeneutical Circle

Catherine Bell provides new insights into the efficacy and transformative power of ritual practices, through the idea of ritualization. The process of ritualization is mainly rooted in the body; specifically, the interaction of the social body (social relations) within a symbolically constituted spatial and temporal environment. Essential to ritualization is the circular production of a ritualized body, which in turn produces ritualized practices. According to Bell, "ritualization is embedded within the dynamics of the body defined within a symbolically structured environment."[26] The interaction between body and social body can be perceived as a hermeneutical circle. According to Schleiermacher, the father of modern hermeneutics, the process of interpretation is circular, constituting the interaction between the "particular" and the "whole."[27] In the process of ritualization, the "particular" corresponds to the individual body, and the "whole" corresponds to the "social body."[27] The interaction between the body and social body is an unending process, and it is not circular in the strict sense; rather, it acts more like a spiral.

Subaltern ritual practices are not theologically and philosophically invalid "superstitious activities." But they are valuable, contributive religious resources which can revolutionize the Christian theological methods and initiate new imaginations about

---

26. Bell, *Ritual Theory, Ritual Practice*, 93.
27. Schleiermacher, *Hermeneutics: The Handwritten Manuscripts*, 168.

the body and social body. Unlike the Enlightenment theoretical tendency to define ritual from a mechanistic/functional way, Post-Enlightenment theory reimagines ritual as embodied practice. The embodied paradigm of ritual challenges to expand the hermeneutical horizon of subaltern theology. The subaltern theology in India should give attention to the "texts" other than the canonical texts. Ritual can be taken as a text, with all its plurivocity. The process of ritualization can be considered as a hermeneutical circle. By considering the subaltern ritual body as a hermeneutical key, new imaginations of the subaltern body and its relation to social body are emphasized. Let me conclude with the words of the late twentieth-century Afro-American writer and founder of the festival of "Kwanzaa,"[28] Maulana Karenga: "Ritual is the primary means for self-transformation and cultural revolution."[29]

---

28. The festival of Kwanzaa is celebrated from December 26th to January 1st. It begins the day after Christmas and ends on New Year's Day. Kwanzaa celebrates the Afro-American people, their culture, and their history. It is a time of reflection and community gatherings. The festival is created by Dr Maulana Ron Karenga in 1966, during a time when Afro-Americans were focused on a struggle to gain equality in America. The very first festival of Kwanzaa was celebrated on the 26th of December, 1966. The purpose of Kwanzaa is to bring everyone together in celebration of their black culture.

29. Bell, *Ritual: Perspectives and Dimensions*, xi.

Chapter 8

Celebrating "Hybridity" and "Memory"
Subaltern Religious Sensibilities in India

"The struggle of [hu]man against power is a struggle of memory against forgetting."[1]

—MILAN KUNDERA

IN INDIA, THE RELIGIOUS realm is always a site of hegemony, negotiation, and boundary crossing. Through mythologizing, re-mythologizing, ritual practicing, and improvising, serious negotiations are happening in the contested religious space of India. In this religio-cultural ecosystem, the Subaltern religious sensibilities produce an embodied difference. It is important to voice and politicize these subaltern religious sensibilities and aesthetics,[2] as

1. Kundera, *Book of Laughter and Forgetting*.
2. This is an argument inspired by Walter Benjamin's work "The Work of Art in the Time of Mechanical Reproduction." He concludes the essay by saying: "This is the situation of politics which Fascism is rendering aesthetic. Communism responds by politicizing art." Benjamin, *Illuminations: Essays and Reflections*, 242.

Celebrating "Hybridity" and "Memory"

a part of postcolonial liberative engagements. Unbundling and uncovering these types of religious aesthetics is a risky and challenging effort as the homogenizing tendency of Hindu fundamentalists is increasing at an alarming rate, and also these religious phenomena seems to keep a conscious ambiguity as a part of its strategic existence. From this vantage point, the primary objective of this paper is to unbundle certain themes involved in subaltern religious sensibilities, particularly the concepts of hybridity and memory. My attempt to explore these ideas will be from a postcolonial perspective, to suggest "hybridity and memory" as a plausible, meaningful, and contested religious and social existence for the subaltern in India.

SUBALTERN RELIGION: RELEVANT OBSERVATIONS

Subaltern religion and culture in India have been considered to be a part of the dominant caste Hindu culture and the polluted part of a purity/pollution ideology. So it is considered to be pejorative from a dominant perspective. But a close observation reminds us of the subversive and contested characteristics of subaltern religious experience as a cultural representation of the subaltern people in India. It is multifarious and plural in nature.

The Symbolic World of Subaltern Religion

The symbolic representations of subaltern religion provide lenses with which to view and frame and organize the plethora of Dalit cultural and religious symbols. The symbolic representation of the goddess Ellaiyamman is characterized by its distinctiveness. Unlike the classical Hindu tradition, the goddess is "independent" without having any attestation or authorization from any male god.[3] It is important to note that in the Dalit religion, goddesses

---

3. In Classical Hindu tradition, the female goddesses are usually attested and authorized by the corresponding male god. For example, Lakshmi Devi is

are not married. This uncommitted, un-obliged character of the Dalit goddess is a break with the Hindu religio-cultural symbolic system of meaning. The other Dalit goddesses, such as *Mariayamman* and *Gangaiamman*, also follow the same tradition of a contested nature. There are continuities and discontinuities. Sati Clarke clarifies that he doesn't want to create binary opposition by putting subaltern religion as a counter to the dominant caste Hindu religion. Rather, he intends to acknowledge the "embodied difference"[4] of Dalit religious life. This embodied difference makes the subaltern peoples' collective life possible. By reflecting upon the Dalit religious symbolic representations, one can conclude that subaltern religion and culture as a whole is a constructed system of collective representation.

Multimodalities of Subaltern Religious Life

Subaltern religion and culture share a multi-modal existence. To acknowledge the various modes of subaltern reflexivity, we need to broaden our horizons. There is a dominant "logocentric" attitude in religious studies in India, which postulate an intellectual primacy to the act of writing. But subaltern religious life surpasses these traditional conceptions. According to the Indian Folklorist Chitrasen Pasayat, folklores (which consist of the religious and cultural life of Dalits and tribals) should be studied from a holistic perspective, considering their multidimensionality:

> Folklore is commonly believed to be the oral literature that is handed down to us from generation to generation through oral tradition. It incorporates folk songs, folk dances, folk tales, superstitions, myths, etc. But the scope of folklore is much wider. It includes material and non-material, verbal and nonverbal cultures. Therefore, an attempt to study cultures in its real sense should

---

perceived as the wife of Vishnu, Parvathy as the wife of Siva . . . Sita to Rama and so on. See Brown, *The Triumph of the Goddess: The Canonical Models and Theological Visions of the Devi-Bhagavata Purana*, 94.

4. Clarke, *Subaltern Culture*, 96.

thereof include an analysis of agriculture and agrarian history, settlement patterns, dialectology of folk speech, folk architecture, folk cookery, folk costumes, the notion of time in folk society, folk literature, folk play, folk arts, and crafts.[5]

There are numerous modes of subaltern religious expressions like symbols, myths, rituals, icons, body movements, art, architecture, sacred geography, music, etc. They should all be considered as textualities. Through cultural and religious acts like drumming, dancing, weaving, painting, and making artifacts, the subaltern contains the shape and express their reflections. Thus the religious reflexivity of the subaltern people not only surpasses literacy and orality but also challenges those constructions.

SUBALTERN RELIGION AS HYBRID RELIGION

The subaltern religion borrows from the caste Hindu symbolic system, and also from other religious traditions by contextual needs, with an aim to debunk or transfigure them for subaltern purposes. This politics of manipulation happens implicitly, through keeping its "liminality" (in between-ness) untouched by the dominant. It is interesting to note that the subaltern religious sensibilities are not trying to forge a completely brand-new, counter-religious identity in opposition to the caste Hinduism, as we observed earlier. But conscious improvisations, subversive imaginations, contested practices are at the heart of subaltern religion. Here the notion of hybridity, popularized by Homi K. Bhabha, serves as a hermeneutical tool for analyzing the subaltern religious sensibilities to makes sense of these ambiguities, and also to genuinely attempt to understand them beyond dualisms. In the words of Bhabha:

> Hybridity is a problematic of colonial representation and individuation that reverses the effects of the colonialist disavowal, so that other "denied" knowledges enter upon

5. Pasayat, *Tribe, Caste and Folk Culture*, 13.

the dominant discourse and estrange the basis of its autonomy—its rules of recognition.[6]

The process of hybridity points to the crossing-over of boundaries of the dominant/colonial space by incorporating some of its values and accomplishments, and also intruding into the hegemonic space without being controlled by the dominant. This characteristic of hybridization is explicitly seen in the subaltern religious phenomena. Subaltern religion consciously intrudes into the symbolic world of Hinduism's caste system, and challenges its authority. From a theological point of view, Vebjorn L. Horsfjord reflects upon this subaltern religious sensibility in India by affirming the idea of the "polyvalence of cultural and religious expressions and hybridity" in subaltern religious engagements.[7] So, it is well evident that subaltern religion is a hybrid religion.

Ellaiyamman: The Construction of a Subaltern Myth

Etymologically, "Ellaiyamman" means the "mother of all beings." The word "*Ellai*" has two meanings. In one sense it refers to "all," and on the other hand, it points to the "border." So there are two interpretative possibilities: one as goddess of all beings and the other as the goddess of the border. The strategic position of the Ellaiyamman icon is on the border of the village. This border, or liminal space, serves as a third space of contestation.

Apparently, the story seems to be a traditional Hindu mythological setting.[8] The plot of the story itself is rooted in the Hindu mythological/symbolic world. By making use of Hindu metaphors and mythological characters, the subaltern myth is getting attention in the religious landscape. The mythological names like Brahma, Prasurama, Gandharva, and Narada are familiar Hindu names in South India. The concepts of chastity and purity (and

6. Bhabha, *The Location of Culture*, 175.

7. Horsfjord, "Challenging Contexts," 54.

8. For an elaborative explanation of the story of the Ellayamman, refer to Sahi, "Seeds of Tradition," 95.

sacrifice on behalf of chastity) are all closely related to the Hindu idea of the ideal. The metaphor of the devout/faithful wife named Renuka is a stereotyped Hindu concept of a housewife, according to the Hindu dharma[9].

An important dimension of this myth is its symbolic inversion, through projecting a hybrid representation of the goddess Yellamma, the hybrid god having a Dalit head and Brahmin body! It is undoubtedly subversive in the religio-symbolic world of India. According to the Hindu caste hierarchy, Brahmins are the embodiment of wisdom and knowledge, and the outcastes are the so-called "untouchables" and complacent, always being in the material realm. But the myth reinstates and transfigures the social order by repositioning the accepted order of the social body. By reimagining the divine body, it reorders the social body.

Hybridization as Cautious Symbiosis

In the subaltern mythographies, one cannot find a pure/counter subaltern move against the dominant from a dualistic point of view. And the subaltern religious phenomenon in India is not forging a brand new religious sect, as most of the "converted Christians" do. But an apparent strategic distancing from the dominant is visible and commendable. By using the available resources, the dominant and the subaltern—and in some particular situations other religious resources like Islamic Sufi resources (e.g., dargahs in rural Andhra Pradesh)—the subaltern people are making and celebrating hybridity as a plausible and meaningful social existence. It is a process of symbiosis, which involves a cautious give and takes. This can be further explained by another image, that of a "junk salesman." The junk salesman is the one who collects everything from the houses and sells whatever is valuable. The material that has no value will be stored in a corner. But eventually he takes the unused materials and assembles it together to make something

9. Hindu dharma refers to the ordained duty of each person in the society. Dharma is intrinsically connected to the caste system, which is the basis of discrimination.

useful for his purpose. Nothing is wasted. Using his discernment and practical intelligibility, the junk salesman puts everything together to make life plausible and meaningful. This is similar to the subaltern religious sensibility, which uses all the available religious resources to forge the subaltern collective subjectivity.

Mimicry, Deception, and Survivability

A sort of mimicry can be sensed in the subaltern religion: mimicking the dominant. The use of mythological characters, metaphors, etc., is evidence of this mimicry. This idea of mimicry is always deceptive because it resembles the dominant, but it is deviant at its core. By making such resembling and complacent adaptations, the subaltern people make a hardcore difference which is not visible and not easy to be found. Keeping this ambiguity untouched by the dominant, the subaltern religion succeeds to deceive the dominant from attacking back. Howard Thurman also uses this idea of deception in the same sense of dissimulation, observing that "deception is perhaps the oldest of all the techniques by which the weak have protected themselves against the strong."[10] Through this, they can survive. So hybridity and mimicry is the survival kit for the subaltern people.

CELEBRATING MEMORY: PRATHYAKSHS RAKSHA DAIVA SABHA

"Prathyakhsha Rakasha Daiva Sabha" (God's Church of Visible Salvation) is a Dalit religious sect in Central Kerala, founded by Poykayil Yohannan in 1910. This initiative of Yohannan's emerged out of the strong disinterest and protest against Christianity, to which many Dalit people converted in the twentieth century, with the arrival of Church Missionary Society missionaries. The converted Dalit Christians were vehemently discriminated against by many within the church in the name of their caste and color. This

10. Thurman, *Jesus and the Disinherited*, 58.

made Yohannan establish an independent religion by mobilizing the Parayas, Pulayas, and similar Dalit communities in Kerala. The new religious sect combined ideas of salvation and spiritual progress along with social and economic development. The movement gave equal emphasis to the spiritual and material dimensions of life, especially significant in the context of Dalit communities that were battling the centuries-old caste slavery. According to Sanal Mohan, "Yohannan imaginatively created a hybrid religion by combining several elements of Christian discourses and practices with elements drawn from the Dalit life-world."[11] The unique use of ritual practices, which re-memorialized the slave experience, was at the heart of this religion. By ritually celebrating the painful memory of caste slavery, this religious sect forged an emancipatory discourse on history. In Yohannan's writings, the lack of history for the slave people is problematized:

> I behold the histories of many races
> Every History in Karalam was searched for.
> There was nothing written on my race,
> There was not on the earth to write the story of my race
> And it was drowned in the abysmal
> Darkness of the nether world.[12]

Through his songs and discourses, Yohannan vehemently problematized the issue of representation. It was in the lacuna of a proper political representation for Dalits that the ritual re-memory of the history is religiously and politically placed by Yohannan. Through remembrance of the historical past, the need for representation is meaningfully introduced. Thus, the new religion has become a third space where hybridity, memory, and representation were celebrated.

Both the notions of "hybridity" and "memory" are very relevant categories and tools for meaningful subaltern theological engagements in India. With the homogenizing tendency of Hindu cultural nationalism, along with the neo-colonial forces

11. Mohan, *Modernity of Slavery*, 152.
12. Ibid., 276.

of globalization looming large, the celebration of hybridity and memory can become the weapon of the oppressed. Hybridity is the theological urgency of the day, as Horsfjord says: "For a theology to be meaningful, it must never be so closed into one symbol system that it cannot be understood by anyone else. This is close to requiring an element of hybridity in any theology."[13] The idea of ritual re-memory of subaltern history resonates across different indigenous cultures. The famous Bolivian historian and social theorist, Silvia Rivera Cusicanqui proposes an idea of "Nayrapacha," which is popular among Bolivian indigenous people, and refers to "the ancient times. But it is not ancient in the sense of a dead past, gone and without importance of renewal. Rather it implies that this world is reversible, that the past can also be the future."[14] Both of these ideas re-affirm the importance of memory for meaningful subaltern theological engagements. Womanist Theologian Iva E. Carruthers reminds us of the *Sankofa* Bird in West Africa,[15] whose beak touches its tail as a reminder of the circle of life. It is a call to look back to move forward. For an oppressed community, it is very meaningful to remember the past. As Milan Kundera so beautifully states it; 'the struggle of [hu]man against power is a struggle of memory against forgetting.'[16]

13. Horsfjord, "Challenging Contexts," 54.
14. Mignolo, *Local Histories/Global Designs*, 172.
15. Hopkins and Thomas, *Walk Together Children*, 300.
16. Kundera, *Book of Laughter and Forgetting*.

Chapter 9

"Sacred Grove"
Reclaiming a Subaltern Paradigm for Ecological Restoration

> "Embrace our trees
> Save them from being felled
> The property of our hills
> Save it from being looted."[1]
> —Ghanshyam Raturi, Indian Poet

> "I believe in the forest, and in the meadow, and in the night in which the corn grows. Life consists with wildness. The most alive is the wildest."[2]
> —Henry David Thoreau

In India, there is specifically a religious "affection" towards the forest. From ancient seers to the Buddha, a broad spectrum of divine subjectivities have communed deeply with nature. The notion

---

1. Shiva, *Staying Alive*, 73.
2. Highland, *Meditations of Henry David Thoreau*, 98.

of spiritual enlightenment is also connected to the practice of being in communion with nature. Buddha and many other seers experienced their enlightenment while meditating (*tapas*) under the shadow of trees. In fact, Buddha is said to have meditated under a great banyan tree which is still preserved and protected in West Bengal. The connection between enlightenment and trees/forest is very deep and is found at the heart of the indigenous/subaltern spirituality in India. This religious sensibility towards trees and forests can be traced back to the tradition of the "sacred grove" of the indigenous people in India. I would like to call these people of modern India "a subaltern collective."[3] The objective of this paper is to reclaim the subaltern religious practice of the sacred grove tradition as a paradigm of ecological resistance and restoration.

SACRED GROVE: DEFINITIONS

Sacred groves are the patches of forest that are protected, preserved, and considered to be sacred. These protected forest patches have survived periods of deforestation, political turmoil, and natural calamities because there existed a strong conservation ethos coupled with taboos and traditions. Vartak and Gadgil define these sacred groves:

> Specific areas imbued with powers beyond those of humans; they are home to mighty spirits that can take or give life. They originate from a range of roots and include: sites linked to specific events; sites surrounding

---

3. The term "subaltern" is used repeatedly and often contextualized in this paper. The term was popularized by the Italian Marxist Antonio Gramsci, to denote non-elite or subordinated social groups. This term gained importance in India after the work of a group of thinkers, usually referred to as the Subaltern Studies Collective. Between 1982 and 1996, the Subaltern Collective has published nine volumes on South Asian history and society. In the preface to the first volume, *Subaltern Studies*, Ranajit Guha proposes "subaltern" as a generic term to refer to "the general attribute of subordination in South Asian societies irrespective of its expression regarding class, caste, age, gender, and office or in any other way" (Guha, Preface to *Subaltern Studies*, vii). An extended critique of the notion of subaltern is advanced by Gayatri Chakravorty Spivak. See Spivak, "Subaltern Studies: Deconstructing Historiography," 330–363.

temples; burial grounds or cemeteries housing the spirits of the ancestors; the homes of protective spirits; the homes of deities from which priests derive their healing powers; homes to a powerful animal or plant species; forest areas that surround natural sacred features such as rivers, rocks, caves[sic] and "bottomless" water holes and sites of initiation or ritual.[4]

This pan-Indian phenomenon is closely connected to the folklore traditions and ritual practices. It is a complex cultural phenomenon interlinked with socio-religious and economic factors of the people's lives in their particular contexts. Eliza F. Kent observes that these forest patches are to be considered as relics in both botanical and cultural terms. She says, "They not only preserved remnant patches of old-growth forest that used to cover the subcontinent; they also harbored primitive forms of religiosity that had been long superseded by *Brahmanical* Hinduism, Islam, Christianity, and other more modern religions."[5]

The sacred groves are known by various names in India: such as "Kaavu" in Kerala, "Devara Kadu" in Karnataka, "Koil Kaadu" in Tamil Nadu, "Sarnas" in Madhya Pradesh, "Deorali" in Darjeeling and so on. The religious beliefs and practices around "sacred grove" are varied and contextual. But all of them share commonalities, especially regarding the religious taboos which play a significant role in preserving them.

SACRED GROVE: MULTI-PERSPECTIVAL APPROACH

The sacred grove tradition is a multifarious phenomenon which demands a multidimensional approach to its study. Thus, the scientific, ecological, religious, folklorist, historical, and sociological dimensions of the sacred grove should be explored to understand its environmental value for modern society. There are several social scientists and folklorists who consider the sociological

4. Gadgil and Vartak, "Sacred Groves of India," 314.
5. Kent, *Sacred Groves and Local Gods*, 4.

and cultural importance of "sacred groves" in the Indian context. Folklorists like K. K. N. Kuruppu and Raghavan Payyanad point to the cultural politics of the sacred grove tradition, which is closely connected to a subaltern ritual practice of "Theyyam"[6] in North Kerala. Gadgil and Vartak and other eco-scientists reinstate the ecological importance of the sacred grove tradition in an age of deforestation and ecological crisis. Thus, the sacred grove is a multi-dimensional and multifarious phenomenon, which needs a careful interdisciplinary study to unearth its importance.

Embodiment of Subaltern Religious Sensibility

Sacred groves are the embodiments of subaltern religiosity in India. They are centers of folklores, beliefs, and taboos. The "Kavus," the sacred groves of Kerala, are considered to be a place to worship gods and goddesses. The religious origin of sacred groves is from the practice of tree worship. In India, nature is considered as the symbol of mother goddess (Bhoo Devi). The worship of mother goddess has a substantial existence in India.

Mythical Dimension

Tree lore is a standard feature of subaltern religiosity. The metaphor of "the tree of life," or the "Axis Mundi," is featured by the Sarna religion in India. Sarna is the name of a tribal group in Jharkhand state. The name itself refers to the sacred grove. Nowadays, the tribal people in Central-East India—particularly the Munda, Ho, Santal, and Khuruk—have reclaimed their religion as "Sarna Dorom," the religion of the sacred woods. This is a response to the attempt within the Hindu fundamentalist movement to subsume the subaltern religious sensibilities into the dominant Hindu fold. In Sarna Dorom there are many mythical elements related to the

---

6. "Theyyam" is a subaltern ritual dance in North Malabar. It is a worship culture of the Dalit people, and a differentiated form of religion compared to the idol worship of caste Hinduism.

trees. They worship the god Dharmesh, who is embodied in the "Sal" tree. They also worship Chalapacho Devi, the mother goddess who is embodied in nature. The Sal tree is considered as a totem, in which the spirits of Chalapacha Devi and Dharmesh are manifested.[7] So, the Sal tree is symbolized as a "cosmic tree" or the Axis Mundi in the Sarna religion.

In Kerala, the woods are believed to be the representations of ancestors' spirits and the abode of gods and goddesses, especially in the Kavus. Ecologically, the idea that the gods and goddesses live in or beneath huge trees contributes significantly to the movement to protect the whole landscape from erosion. In Wayanad,[8] where indigenous people like the Paniya and Kurichiar mostly live, a popular tree lore is celebrated and given religious significance. "The myth of a chained tree" is a very familiar story relating to tree worship in Wayanad. At the entrance to the Wayanad district, there is a sacred grove on the side of the road where the local people worship a banyan tree which is believed to be the embodiment of the spirit of an ancestor named Karinthandan. Karinthandan was a tribal man who helped the British colonizers to find their way inside the deep forest of Wayanad during the colonial period. After discovering the unknown routes in the thick forest with the help of the native informant Karinthandan, the British officers shot him dead. But the soul of Karinthandan was said to have haunted the colonizers and other passengers on that particular route to Wayanad. The tree that is believed to be the embodiment of Karinthandan's spirit is worshipped by the passengers to avoid bad omens and problems.[9] In addition to being re-read as an anti-colonial resistance, this story is also part of an eco-resistant indigenous religious sensibility against unsustainable modern development.

---

7. "Sarnaism," Wikipedia, https://en.wikipedia.org/wiki/Sarnaism.

8. Wayanad is a northern district of Kerala, in India. It is a place geographically located in the Northeastern part of the Western Ghats and where the indigenous tribal people like the Paniya and Kurichiar are mostly inhabited.

9. Raj, *Childhood Stories*, 1.

Ritual Dimension

Specifically, Sarna religious rituals are intimately related to the Sal tree (*Shorea robusta*) worship. The Sal tree is considered as the universal mother, Sarna Mata. The Sarna people offer devotional care to this tree along with other plants in the sacred groves. The religious worship and rituals are varied and improvised within each village. The worship is conducted officially by the village priest,. called "pahan." The women also perform the religious ritual on a daily basis. They consider the Sal tree as their "Sarna Mata."[10] Because it is believed that the Mata was very disappointed to find that the sacred groves are deteriorating, the Sarna people began to plant new Sal saplings and protect them by surrounding the saplings with wooden gates.

"Theyyam" is another indigenous belief system with many ecological implications. Theyyam and associated rituals are typically performed in the sacred groves of northern Kerala. This tradition is intrinsically related to hero/heroine worship, which is performed mainly in the sacred groves. The use of archetypal and ecological symbols like the symbol of sacred place, the symbolism of the tree, the symbol of animal, symbol of fertile earth, fire, etc., mark the symbolic relation between humans and nature in Theyyam. The elements of tree worship, the fertility cult in Theyyam, signify the symbiotic relationship between human and nature. The worship at Kavus, the sacred groves, is the visible sign of the preservation and the care of the ecosystem through ritual means. The Kavus are considered to be the abode of gods and goddesses. A cosmology grounded on ecology provides the rationale for a symbiotic relation with nature.

EMBODIMENT OF SUBALTERN ECO-SCIENCE

The sacred groves can be perceived as an expression of subaltern eco-science. It serves as an "abode of biodiversity" constituted by

---

10. Sarna Mata is a pre-Sanskrit concept of the divine, which attributes divinity to the mother earth. See Borde, "The Devi as Ecofeminist Warrior," 271.

several rare species of animals and plants. The medicinal plants found in sacred groves are used by the practitioners of village medicine (usually called "ayurveda"). The sacred grove also works as a system of eco-preservation.

Biological Diversity

The heavily protected sacred groves provide a real picture of the biodiversity of the earth. Nothing is ever removed from the groves; not a twig, not even a fallen branch. No one is permitted to cut any tree or plant, kill animals and birds, or do any harm to any form of life in the grove. As a result of the high level of conservation, biodiversity is maintained in the sacred groves. The sacred groves remain secure places for many endangered species of flora and fauna. Jithesh Maniyath refers to an eco-folklore study on the sacred groves of Northern Kerala. According to him, the only bird from Kerala which is found in the Red Data Book is the white-bellied sea eagle, which can only be seen in some of the sacred groves of North Kerala, specifically Edayilekkadu Kavu.[11] Several rare species of medicinal plants have been found in the interior part of sacred groves, where human beings have still not reached. In this way, then, the sacred groves provide an organic space of biodiversity.

Conservation Model

Madhav Gadgil is the first environmental scientist in India to write passionately about the ecological significance of sacred groves. According to Gadgil, sacred groves are "ecologically significant refuge for species."[12] Gadgil's experiments with protozoa demonstrated that one could prevent the extinction of prey species only by providing them with an area inaccessible to predators, from whence they could repopulate and colonize other areas, by placing them

11. Maniyath, "Forests of Belief," 30.
12. Gadgil and Guha, *This Fissured Land*, 24.

in an environment where no limits were put on the population of either prey or predator.[13] Sacred groves serve as such a shelter for animals and plants. Especially the huge trees, like the banyan and the pipal, which are considered to be sacred, and which function as an abode for several microorganisms, birds, and plants. As an ecosystem, the sacred grove exists as a conservation system. It gives adequate irrigation and fertility to the earth. One of the significant resources that is being conserved by sacred groves is water. Sacred groves serve as a reservoir of pure water, and they also generate new streams of water. Several studies have been done by scholars researching the intrinsic connection of sacred groves and water resources. As an ecosystem, the environmental significance of the sacred grove is evident in the stellar role they play in soil and water conservation. Most of the sacred groves also have sacred water bodies, springs, ponds, lakes, streams, and rivers. These recharge the water reservoirs. By preserving such sacred patches of the forest, we can protect our valuable water resources, since water will be a rare resource shortly. However, despite their ecological significance, the sacred groves are not considered as a scientific eco-conservation model by the Indian Forest Ministry, as they depend more on the religious and cultural aspects of the local communities concerning their preservation and sustenance. But it is more meaningful to put it as Gadgil does: an exemplary system of "traditional community resource management."[14]

Edge of Extinction

The sacred taboos related to sacred groves work as protective tools for its preservation purpose. But modern changes in beliefs and ethos influenced this new generation, and they don't care about such archaic beliefs. Discarding such ancient religious practices as irrational usually ends up devaluing the ecological significance of the sacred groves. The modern notion of dualism is also working

13. Ibid, 24.
14. Ibid.

behind this eco-negligence. The divide between mind/body, culture/nature, theory/practice, male/female, urban/village, civilized/savage, and domestic/wild; such homologies are also imprinted in people's attitude towards nature. Aryanisation[15] is another significant problem. Due to the vehement influence of Hindu nationalist groups, ancient sacred groves are being transformed into temples. When temples replace sacred groves, it replaces the ecosystem too. The construction of Talacauveri temple in Coorg is a recent example of the destruction of a sacred grove.

The spirit of urbanization has caused a lot of deforestation in the name of constructing new buildings. We need to think about the real-estate land mafia in India, which is looming large as a demon, has made an enormous negative impact. They consciously facilitate the land trade and grab sacred groves for building shopping complexes and five-star restaurants. Sacred spaces like Kavus have become a valuable product in the market economy now. Here, we can sense a "tradition versus modernity" dialectic and its problem. In fact, sacred groves are at the edge of extinction, which demands immediate attention.

Ecological Ethnicities and Embodiment of People's Struggle: Some Models

The subaltern religious sensibilities in India are closely connected to the people's struggle for justice and ecological restoration. As the destruction of forests and sacred groves is increasing at an alarming rate, several local communities and individuals protect them. We can find a broader subaltern collective of people in India, who are committed to ecology and its preservation. The eco-scientists Frederique A. Marglin and Pramod Parajuli rightly name this subaltern collective of people as "ecological ethnicities."[16] These ecological ethnicities include peasants, fisher folks, tribal, forest

---

15. "Aryanisation" is a conscious political act of the Hindu fundamentalists to hold Dalit and tribal people and their cultures in the Hindu fold by homogenizing all the little traditions in India.

16. Marglin and Parajuli, *Sacred Grove and Ecology*, 296.

dwellers, nomadic shepherds and a host of people marginalized by development projects. Some of the signposts of the people's struggle for eco-justice are given below, and I think they are the embodiment of subaltern eco-resistant spirituality.

The Bishnois Community

The Bishnois are a small subaltern ethnic group in the state of Rajasthan, India. They practice environmental conservation on an everyday basis as their religious duty. The Bishnois believe that cutting a tree or killing a bird or animal is sacrilege. The Bishnoi religion was founded by Guru Maharaj Jambaji, born in 1451 CE.[17] The Marwar area was the place where Bishnois inhabited, and very vulnerable to the extreme climatic conditions. Once, Marwar succumbed to severe drought. The young Maharaj Jambaji witnessed the difficulties of the drought and noticed that the people cut down trees to feed animals; when the drought continued, nothing was left to feed the animals and resulted in their deaths. Jambaji thought that if trees were protected, animal life would be sustained, and his community would survive. So he formulated twenty-nine injunctions. The injunctions banned the cutting of any green tree or killing of any animals. The community practiced these injunctions religiously and passionately. The geographical area transformed into a land of dense forest after an extended period. Later, the king of Jodhpur wanted to uproot the Bishnoi community so that he could build a new palace using the timber from the Bishnoi forests. The people protested against this attempt, and the king's soldiers attacked the Bishnoi community. The people protested by encircling each tree with their bodies, led by a Bishnoi woman. Finally, the king heard about the Bishnoi-religious custom of protecting the trees and environment, and he released an official order to protect the Bishnoi beliefs and customs. Even today the Bishnoi community continues to protect trees and animals. This became an inspiration for the Chipko movement in 1973.

17. Dwivedi, *Dharmic Ecology*, 16.

Chipko Movement

The Chipko Movement was launched in March of 1973 as a result of a protest of the villagers in the town of Gopeshwar in Chamoli district, Uttar Pradesh. They formed a human chain and encircled the trees to keep them from being felled. The cutting of the trees was intended for manufacturing sports equipment in a nearby factory. This repeated in another village as a powerful resistance against the forest contractors who wanted to cut the trees illegally. Also, in 1974 women from the village of Reni near Joshimath in the Himalayas protested logging by hugging trees, forcing the contractors to leave. Since then, the Chipko Movement has continued to grow from a grassroots "eco-development movement."[18]

The Chipko Movement is not only an embodiment of subaltern religious sensibilities, but also its ecological and economic concerns. Peasants and indigenous people, who are more vulnerable to ecological crisis and climatic changes, are more conscious and aware of the fact that the industrial and commercial demands have been the cause of deforestation. They are acutely aware of their vulnerability regarding the removal of livelihood in a deforested area. Floods and droughts continue to play a vital role in the uprooting of the simple folks like peasants and tribal people. Specifically, women are more vulnerable to the ecological crisis, as they are the individuals who have to manage the natural resources like firewood, water, and domestic animals. Most of the time they have to walk miles in search of firewood and water. The Chipko Movement powerfully problematizes this feminist dimension of eco-crisis too. In this sense, the movement can be considered a women's movement in India.

Sarna Mata Movement

East-Central India is an abode of several sacred groves traditionally owned by the tribal people like the Santals, Oarons, and Munda. The people believed that these sacred groves house the goddess Sarna

18. Bhatt, *Chipko Movement*, 17.

Mata. The poor indigenous women, very affected by the destruction of the sacred groves, which are the sources of firewood, water, and other resources, initiated a movement for protecting the sacred groves called the Sarna Mata Movement. The move is aimed at the recreation and regeneration of the sacred groves. This is very related to the religious ritual of the possession trance dance of the indigenous women, who are considered the embodiments of the deity Sarna Mata. During the possession trance, the deity usually commands to protect the sacred groves. Nowadays the women intelligibly use this religious notion very positively to recreate the destroyed groves. Ritual planting of Sal trees is conducted by the self-help groups of these women. Moreover, the self-help groups gather periodically in the sacred groves for discussing their plans and programs. This self-help groups have become a platform of micro-financing, micro-enterprising of manufacturing, and the sale of handmade objects. The movement is getting support from some of the non-governmental organizations in India. According to Radhika Borde, this movement has given birth to "a new feminist consciousness with enormous discursive impact, leading to more widespread nature conservation in rural East-Central India."[19]

Narmada Bachao Andolan (NBA)

NBA is an embodiment of people's struggle against the government policy of building up a massive dam across the Narmada river, deforesting a vast geographical area, and uprooting the tribal people in the state of Madhya Pradesh. With the leadership of Medha Patkar, the environmental activist, people gathered and consolidated their power of resistance against such a blind model of modern development. This people's movement is called "Narmada Bachao Andolan," or "NBA". This has initiated several other people's movement in India and eco-resistance. Such coalitions of ecological ethnicities from different parts of the country have launched a subaltern paradigm of eco-resistance for preserving

---

19. Borde, "The Devi as Ecofeminist Warrior," 279.

ecological resources and natural habitats of biodiversity. NAPM (National Alliance of People's Movement) is an example of a greater platform of solidarity between the people who are fighting for eco-preservation and sustainable development. Tribals and Dalit people are contributing to these alliances for justice and peace for the earth. Subaltern-identified liberationists and liberation-identified subaltern people are the core people in the struggle for eco-justice in India.

These are but a few examples of people's struggle for justice and peace in India, which have become embodiments of subaltern spirituality of resistance and eco-sensitivity.

Re-reading the Sacred Grove as the Subaltern Paradigm of Eco-Restoration

The sacred grove tradition should be re-read as a subaltern paradigm in the present political context of India. The Hindu nationalist movements[20] are purporting a homogenized brahminic cultural hegemony over the subaltern religious and cultural sensibilities. The subaltern eco-ethnicities and their struggles challenge this homogenizing tendency which is sponsored by corporates, as well as the modern unsustainable development model being employed in India. The eco-ethnic communities and their collective bring new discourses on religion, science, and ecological restoration to the table.

---

20. This refers to the Hindu fundamentalist approach of Vishva Hindu Parishad (VHP) and its wings, such as BJP (the political wing) and R.S.S (the religious wing), who believe that India is a Hindu country and practice religious intolerance. Hindu fundamentalists are against the minorities, such as dalits, tribals, Christians, and Muslims. Hindu Cultural Nationalism is programmed religious-political domination for homogenizing Indian culture and vanishing, smaller traditions like subaltern.

Redefining the Sacred Grove as the "Third Space."

The word "sacred" in "sacred grove" challenges all modern notions of the term. According to subaltern spirituality and its practice, the sacred is housed in the earth, the sky, and the whole universe. There is no separatism in this subaltern consciousness, and this consciousness of wholeness dismantles modern dualistic notions of sacred and profane, culture and nature, man and woman, civilized and savage, etc. Usually, the geographical space shared by the sacred groves is "in between" or "liminal"; on the roadside, at the entrance of a village, in between the village and city, in between the home and the temple, etc. This element of "liminality" effectively serves as a "third space" of self-reflexivity, meditation, and commune with nature. In this third space, the modern notions of dualities are collapsed in the everyday life of the devotee. Theoretically speaking, this third space is a place of negotiation and transgression of these modern dualistic tendencies in the consciousness of the people.

Reclaiming Eco-Resistance and Eco-Restoration

The sacred grove has become a powerful subaltern cultural symbol of eco-resistance and eco-restoration in India. The important thing is that we cannot separate this cultural symbol from their struggle for survival and justice. Interestingly, this cultural and political symbol of the sacred grove brings an alternative way of doing eco-science and ecological restoration. Ecological restoration is the attempt to heal the land and make the human relationship to nature whole. As the restoration ecologist Gretel Van Wieren writes, ecological restoration is rooted "in its metaphysical understanding of the fundamental interconnectedness of life and culture and in its practice that provides an experiential bridge between people and land."[21] In effect, the people and communities are restored to the land. From this point of view, the sacred grove tradition is an efficient model of eco-restoration in its practice,

---

21. Van Wieren, *Restored to Earth*, 2.

especially at a local level. The power of such local eco-practices is well-acknowledged. There is a significant cultural resonance between people, specifically regarding these types of eco-practices. The Green Belt Movement founded by the Nobel Prize winner Wangari Maathai is another example for eco-restoration. She defines ecological restoration on a broader level in connection with the struggle for survival. According to Maathai, "eco-restoration is a part of a larger mission to create a society that respects democracy, decency, adherence to the rule of law, human rights, and the rights of women."[22]

Thus the subaltern practice of the sacred grove becomes an uncanny paradigm of ecological restoration because of its micro-level implementation and holistic approach. The sacred grove is an ecosystem, so the restoration of sacred groves results in the sustenance of the whole ecosystem. This subaltern religious sensibility is a model of spirituality which interlinks theory and practice, culture and nature, and religion and science. The sacred grove paradigm is a model of healing, as well. The Hebrew concept of "Tikkun Olam" is very much related to this idea. Tikkun Olam refers to the repairing of the world, or co-creating with the Divine. Rosenthal says that the idea stresses "the role of humans in mending the flaws in creation, healing the cracks, and redeeming the sparks of divinity scattered throughout the world."[23] From this perspective, one can say that sacred groves are the places of holistic healing.

Towards Embedded Ecologies

The subaltern paradigm of the sacred grove provides a comprehensive method of converging religious, cultural, political, and economic worlds for an authentic green shift today. Such convergences embody the "embedded ecologies." By embedded ecologies, I mean the theory and practice of "embedded-ness" which emerges through an "exploration of subtle and complex

---

22. Maathai, *The Green Belt Movement*, 111.
23. Rosenthal, "Tikkun Ha-Olam," 240.

relationships between the cultural and natural worlds."[24] This concept of embedded ecology is an alternative and counter-practice to the modern intentionalities of dis-embedded life. Sacred grove as a subaltern model of eco-restoration is, as previously stated, a converging point of several elements, such as religion, science, culture, economy, and politics. Unbundling such eco-traditions and practices in our religion and culture is a mark of hope and risk.

The sacred grove tradition in India is a powerful subaltern symbolic paradigm of ecological restoration. By preserving biodiversity, the water, and other natural resources, the sacred grove remains as a sign of hope at our ecological tipping point. The modern tendency to demean these indigenous traditions as "superstitious" and "archaic," overlooks the ecological importance of the sacred grove. Hence, it is important to reclaim and re-ground such religious resources to make a green shift for a sustainable future. The natural ability of rural peasants and tribal people to preserve the natural world and to live harmoniously with nature ought to be voiced as a part of their struggle for justice and peace. At the cutting edge of deforestation, the sacred grove tradition exists as a green hope for our world. Let me conclude with the words of Mahatma Gandhi: "What we are doing to the forests of the world is but a mirror reflection of what we are doing to ourselves and one another."[25]

---

24. Nagarajan, "Rituals of Embedded Ecologies," 454.

25. "Mahatma Gandhi-Wikiquote," *Wikipedia*, https://en.wikiquote.org/wiki/Mahatma_Gandhi.

Chapter 10

Evolution as Grounding for Hospitality
Interfaith Interrogations

[Hu]man is not only evolved, [s]he is evolving.[1]
—Theodosius Dobzhansky

WE ARE LIVING IN a world of hostility. The militant reactionary movements such as exclusion, separation, fear, and anxiety. etc., are at all-time-high levels today. The disconnect between the "self" and the "other" has elicited a culture of fear and produced gated communities. An inevitable violence of exclusion within the human existence is being taken for granted. In this context, it is the very responsibility of communities of faith to search for meaningful paradigms and practices. Our world today needs practices of hospitality instead of hostility. How can science and religion contribute or promote the practices of hospitality? The objective of this paper is to explore the possibilities of the "Theory of Biological Evolution." The goal is to revisit this theory as the basis to opening

1. Dobzhansky, *Mankind Evolving*, 346.

up new vistas of interfaith relations and to encourage scientific and religious dialogue in a broader context.

EVOLUTION: A THEOLOGICAL RE-VISIT

Charles Darwin's classic work *On the Origin of Species by Means of Natural Selection* was published in 1859. Today, it is one of the most captivating works of historical, philosophical, and scientific research. Darwin's theory of evolution scientifically explains the process and the logical sequencing of life. It also reveals the existence of various forms of biological life. As a scientific theory and meta-narrative, it answers several important questions, like the reasons for biodiversity. It also discusses the similarities and differences among various species, and how biological life survives. The theory of evolution tries to answer the most fundamental questions about life that religion and theology engage. However, it is absorbing to note that Darwin begins the book by referring to a theological task, in the form of a quote from Whewell's *Bridgewater Treatise*. The quote is as follows:

> But about the material world, we can at least go so far as this—we can perceive that events are brought about not by insulated interpositions of Divine power, exerted in each particular case, but by the establishment of general laws.[2]

So one can assume that Darwin is putting beliefs about the material world in a dialogical frame shared with "beliefs about God." This is evident concerning God and his relationship with this world. I would like to argue that Darwin's work has theological intentions. There is always a space for hospitality within the theory that Darwin proposes. Here I would like to explore some theological themes in connection with the spirit of Darwin's theory of evolution.

---

2. Darwin, *The Origin of Species*, 2.

Tree of Life: Argument on Common Origin

Darwin's concept of the "Tree of Life"[3] is a well-constructed model of biological evolution. He speaks about the effects of natural selection on the descendants of a common ancestor. The model explains how the populations of various species change and branch off through a process called transmutation. Over a period of time, populations vary from a common ancestor, creating diversity. The changing climatic conditions also have a role in the difference among populations. This theory affirms that all living species share a common ancestor and that this "common origin" has some theological implications. Gayle Woloschack, comments that "There is a unity that exists in creation that is a direct result of the collective evolution of all of life on earth within the confines of our common yet varied environment."[4] The interconnectedness of all forms of life is a profound theological theme which stems from the theory of evolution. Woloschack continues:

> Life on earth all shares the same elements (Carbon, nitrogen, trace metals), the same processes (cell division, replication and repair of DNA, transcription of RNA, translation of proteins), even the same genetic code. These shared processes are sufficiently complex to make any two living organisms more similar to each other than anything non-living in the universe ... Thus, humankind and every other species share in unity as they evolve into diversity. Both unity and diversity of life have a profound theological significance that is missed if we do not incorporate the theory of biological evolution into our contemplation of Creation.[5]

So here we see how this theory affirms the unity in diversity and suggests some profound theology. After Darwin, the idea of the Tree of Life was analyzed by several other scientists; however, the concept of common origin remains the center of most

---

3. Ibid., 87.
4. Woloschak, "The Compatibility of the Principles of Biological Evolution," 213.
5. Ibid.

scientific viewpoints. To some extent, the Tree of Life refers to a "lack of plan and order" in evolution. But it can be perceived as the unfolding of life itself. A believer can comprehend it as the unfolding of God's plan.

Continuing Creation

In *Origin of Species*, Darwin tries to keep the possibility of mutations and modifications in creation. According to Darwinian Theory, all species "have been modified, so as to acquire that perfection of structure and co-adaption"[6] through natural means and not through separate creation. He discards the possibility of an independent creation of new species, as nature continues the creation process. This is a theologically pregnant subject since cocreation with the universe is a well-affirmed idea in all Eastern religious traditions.

EVOLUTION AND RELIGIOUS COMPATIBILITIES

Having discussed some of the theological implications of biological evolution, I would like to explore the theological compatibility of Eastern religious traditions; namely, Hinduism, Eastern Christianity, and Buddhism. The primary objective here is to explore the compatibilities and sensibilities of Eastern religious traditions by entering into a dialogue with "biological evolution" (and thus with modern science) to create a broader platform for interfaith engagement. For this, I will be exploring the commonalities shared by these religious traditions regarding biological evolution, from a cultural perspective.

Hinduism

Some consonance between modern science and Hindu tradition can be found. Scholars like Varadaraja observe that Hindu

---

6. Darwin, *The Origin of Species*, 66.

concepts of reality "anticipate"[7] modern scientific knowledge. Vedas depicts the creator of the universe as Prajapati (Lord of the people). And, according to Vedas, this creator made three primordial gods: Agni (fire), Vayu (air) and Surya (Sun). Then he made the sky and water. These are all the prerequisites for the origin of life! In this Vedic imagery, one can easily establish the presence of the sun, air, and water for the source of life. Another mysterious parallel between evolution and Hindu thought can be traced in the doctrine of Dasavatara.

Theory of Evolution and Dasavatara Doctrine

Lord Krishna teaches Arjuna the secret of Avatara:

> For whenever of the right
> A languishing appears, son of Bharata,
> A rising up of unright,
> Then I send Myself forth
> For protection of the good
> And for the destruction of evil-doers,
> To make a firm footing for the right
> I come into being in age after age.[8]

Here the word used for righteousness is "Dharma," which means the "order/rhythm of the universe." According to the *Gita*, God's descent happens when the order of the universe (course of life) is at stake. This happens throughout the ages, as needed, "for the protection of the good." The Avatara doctrine is well-explained in the *Bhagavata Purana* with the concept of Dasavatara (which means ten incarnations of God). This concept also has an uncanny parallel with the theory of biological evolution. "Biological evolution is defined as descent with modification."[9] This "descent with modification" is well-illustrated through the Dasavatara concept.

7. Raman, "Traditional Hinduism and Modern Science," 186.
8. Edgerton, *The Bhagavad Gita*, 23.
9. Woloschak, "The Compatibility of the Principles," 209.

The ten Avataras are, namely, Matsya, Koorma, Varaha, Narasimha, Vamana, Parsurama, Rama, Balarama, Krishna, and Kalki.[10] These Dasavataras (ten incarnations of Vishnu) demonstrate evolution in sequential order starting from the "aquatic animal" to "humans." The sequence is as follows;

1. Matsya (Fish)—origin of life in water
2. Koorma (Tortoise)—progression of life from water to land
3. Varaha (Wild Boar)—life in its animal form
4. Narasimha (Man-Lion)—half human, half animal form
5. Vamana (Dwarf)—progression from half-humanness to fullness but incomplete
6. Parasurama (Human with Axe)—representative of stone age human
7. Rama (Human with a Bow and Arrow)—fully human, responsible form of life
8. Balarama (Human with a Plough)—development of agriculture
9. Krishna (Person of Intelligence and Love)—Full expression of self-consciousness, and inner awareness
10. Kalki (Destroyer/Redeemer)—Represents the God-realization; resurrection and en masse spiritual evolution

The biological evolution by natural selection and causal explanation of the change are "mythologically" explained in this sequential order of Avataras. Since the sequential order has similarities with the Tree of Life proposed by Darwin, it is easy to connect the Hindu view of reality with the theory of evolution. Despite both coming from different systems of thought and being developed in various historical contexts, there are several criticisms and reflections regarding the commonalities between the Hindu doctrine of Dasavatara and evolution. According to Varadaraja,

---

10. *Bhagavata Purana*, 1:3.

The *avatara* stories reflect not only biological, but also cultural evolution. Humans have been evolving from wielders of brute force, symbolized by the axe, to proponents of moral principles, and ultimately to agents of deeper truths about the world . . . I have come to see in the mythologies of bygone days much meaning in the context of both biological and cultural evolution.[11]

Jonathan B. Edelmann argues that "the two different systems can be reinterpreted in the light of each other for new understandings of reality."[12] Meera Nanda reminds us that reductionism may happen by the selective interpretation of the Hindu thoughts.[13] However, we cannot bypass the startling parallel between the Hindu view of reality and Biological evolution.

Eastern Christianity

The terrain of science and religious dialogue has been dominated by Western Christianity. However recently, Eastern Christian traditions have gained renewed importance in these conversations. The work 'Science and Eastern Orthodox Church' by Buxhoeveden and Woloschack is an exquisite example of this new focus. The churches of Eastern and Western traditions differ from each other in their theological emphasis. Buxahoeveden, sums it up when he says: 'these differences are reflected in the areas such as anthropology, salvation, and creation.'[14] And these areas have the potential to transform religion-science interactions too. Now, I would like to also focus on the Eastern Christian traditions. The Eastern Christian traditions follow similar worship traditions and liturgies. These traditions share commonalities with the orthodox traditions (like Russian Orthodox Church). While there are no

---

11. Raman, "Traditional Hinduism and Modern Science," 189.

12. Edelmann, *Hindu Theology and Biology*, 61.

13. Bagir, *Science and Religion*, 28.

14. Buxhoeveden and Woloschak, *Science and the Eastern Orthodox Church*, xi.

theologies formulated as creeds or doctrines, the liturgy is considered doctrinal in these churches.

Theistic Evolution

Theistic evolution is the belief that God was and is the cause of biological variations and that God drives evolution towards purposeful ends. Paulose Mar Gregorios explains the idea of theistic evolution in the Eastern Christian tradition. He says:

> The creative energy of God appears to have taken a gradually ascending path, with humanity emerging at the last stage. Nature is making the ascent, as though by step, from the smallest to the things more perfect. But although humankind appeared at the top of the ladder, it is not entirely unrelated to or independent of the rest of the created world.[15]

According to Mar Gregorios, humanity shares the fundamental nature of all creation. But at the same time, it represents a unique element in God's creative process. It is the unique vocation of humanity. Mar Gregorios draws inspiration from the writings of Saint Gregory, the fourth-century church father, and he attributes some notions of evolutionary theory to the theology of Saint Gregory. Mar Gregorios rephrases the core theological theme of Eastern Christianity as "life ascended gradually from plants to the animal to humanity and that human nature incorporates the vegetative, the animal and the rational."[16]

Theosis/Deification

"Theosis," or deification, is one of the major affirmations of Eastern Christianity. The concept of theosis is all about personal evolution. It is considered to be a gift from God in Eastern Christian tradition. Georgios I. Mantzaridis quotes Maximus the Confessor

15. Mar Gregorios, *The Human Presence*, 63.
16. Ibid.

Evolution as Grounding for Hospitality

as follows: "We undergo deification, and do not create it, for it is supernatural."[17] In a liturgical song of the Mar Thoma Syrian Church of Malabar, this deification process is explicitly mentioned. The spiritual evolution of the image and likeness of God is affirmed. It is depicted as a journey from animal likeness to Christ-likeness: "Let us remember those who exhorted us when we were the animal-like. They guided us on the voyage to become Christ-like. And let us follow their footsteps in the journey to completion."[18] The spiritual evolution affirmed here shares similarities with the biological evolution.

These elements of Eastern Christianity are the best resources to reimagine the theory of evolution as a common ground to meet.

Buddhism

The central point of "evolution theory" is the continuing dimension of the evolution process. According to evolutionary biologist Theodosius Dobzhansky, this point is strangely overlooked. He says: "[hu]man is not only evolved, [s]he is evolving. This is a source of hope in the abyss of despair."[19] This dimension of evolution is an important theme in Buddhist philosophical thought. The *Bodhisattva* ideal of Mahayana Buddhism is one of the essential Buddhist doctrines: "A *Bodhisattva* is a highly evolved human being on the way to becoming a Buddha, who is not seeking enlightenment for himself alone but has vowed to help all other beings achieve Buddhahood before he enters into nirvana."[20] The culmination of Buddhist thought is considered to be the Avatamasaka school, which is based on the Avatamsaka Sutra. Capra connects the Avatamaka Sutra and modern physics and says;

> The central theme of the *Avatamsaka* is the unity and interrelation of all things and events; a conception which

---

17. Mantzaridis, *The Deification of Man*, 61.
18. *Selected Hymns and Order of Worship*, 92.
19. Dobzhansky, *Mankind Evolving*, 346.
20. Capra, *The Tao of Physics*, 98.

is not only the very essence of the Eastern world view but also one of the essential elements of the worldview emerging from modern physics.[21]

The Avatamsaka Sutra tells about various stages in the path of awakening. The track begins with Bodhicitta, who wishes to liberate all the conscious beings. Then "the aspiring *Bodhicitta* becomes engaging *Bodhicitta* upon an actual commitment to the *Bodhicitta* vows. With these steps, the practitioner becomes a Bodhisattva."[22] The whole process of evolution undergoes through ten stages (Bhumis). Each step mark advancement in the process of spiritual evolution. The course of the process from the lowest to the compound follows the similar sequential order that we have noticed in Hindu and Eastern Christian thought. So it is evident that Buddhist tradition also shares the "evolutionist" paradigm.

We have been reflecting upon the religious compatibilities of Eastern religious traditions with biological evolution. The arguments are neither polemical nor apologetic in intention. But the intent was to trace the religious resources in India, which are compatible with science. The Eastern religious traditions are overlooked as non-compatible with science, but the reverse is true. Capra comments;

> There is an essential harmony between the spirit of Eastern wisdom and Western science . . . modern physics goes far beyond technology, that the way—or Tao—of physics can be a path with heart, a way to spiritual knowledge and self-realization.[23]

It is evident that the Eastern religious traditions are not only compatible with modern scientific research, but also complementary to each other.

21. Ibid., 99.
22. Gyatso, *Joyful Path of Good Fortune*, 535.
23. Capra, *The Tao of Physics*, 25.

Evolution as a Paradigm of Hospitality:

I think in the Indian context, where we have a definite disconnect between religion and science, that these types of religious resources that we mentioned earlier can be used positively rather than rejecting them as something pejorative. These resources can act as a catalyst to scientific and religious dialogue. The theory of biological evolution can be used as a common platform.

Here, I propose the theory of evolution be viewed as the grounding for hospitality, where scientific and religious dialogue advances further interfaith engagements/relationship in India. Over time, the evolution process has been interpreted as hostile territory by both scientists and theologians. However, it is time to revisit the evolution theory from a hospitality perspective. Recently I read about an interfaith initiative launched by the Global Negotiation Project at Harvard University, which seeks to build a route of cultural tourism following the footsteps of Abraham. The project is known as "Abraham Path."[24] It helps to develop a greater understanding of Judaism, Islam, and Christianity, claiming the common heritage and meeting each other in the Abrahamic footsteps. While the project has had some significant impact and many positive responses, it also has its limitations. For example, it doesn't propose a common ground for everybody; also, it is confined within the religious trio of Judaism, Christianity, and Islam, specifically excluding Hinduism and Buddhism. For a broader vision of interfaith relations, I propose "evolution" as a common meeting place for interfaith relations.

PRACTICING HOSPITALITY: SOME SUGGESTIONS

The practice of hospitality is grounded in the idea of common origin and shared lives as proposed by biological evolution. Since "evolution" is a logical grounding, it can open up a new platform where everybody can come together, including atheists, theists, scientists, priests, philosophers, teachers, students, and so on. This

---

24. Shepherd, *The Gift of the Other*, 251.

practice should initiate interfaith and interdisciplinary engagements, as well as practices for a better world. Some of the practical suggestions are provided in the following sections of this paper.

Hermeneutics Beyond Literalism

Religious scriptures should be re-read from a hospitality perspective, rather than literal interpretation. More specifically, creation narratives should be interpreted in a way that is compatible with science. The recent comments made by Pope Francis regarding the creation story and evolution can be viewed as a positive sign for such an undertaking. The pope stated: "evolution in nature is not opposed to creation because evolution presupposes the creation of beings that evolve."[25] The interpretation of the creation story in Genesis by Sergius Bulgakov is also necessary when he says that the sequence of days in the creation story (Genesis 1) refers to "a gradual or evolutionary actualization of all forms of being."[26]

Interdisciplinary Pedagogy

There is a need to develop interdisciplinary pedagogy for teaching the religious narratives on creation; for example, a revision of the catechism curriculum with an interdisciplinary perspective so that science and religion dialogue can be promoted.

Ecosensitive Community

The idea of the common origin of life and its unity also have profound ecological implications. Woloschock says with firm conviction that:

> Integration helps humanity to see the relationship of all creatures, indeed our relationship with the earth itself.

25. McKenna, "Pope Francis: 'Evolution . . . Is Not Inconsistent with the Notion of Creation,'" para. 1.
26. Bulgakov, *The Bride of the Lamb*, 173.

Evolution as Grounding for Hospitality

The diversity of creation helps to understand the need for all creatures, all of life, all niches and environments to support each other and our planet. With both of these concepts come a profound ecological consciousness and a view of humans as priests of creation.[27]

The recent ecological problems in India[28] remind us to re-assert this unity and the interconnectedness of all creation. Local parishes/neighborhoods should be re-established as eco-friendly communities that initiate sustainable practices.

Science as Interfaith Practice

Science and technology can also be re-established as interfaith practices in the Indian context. The implementation of technological innovations for the common interest at the local level without considering religious divisions and differences can foster interfaith relationships within the community. Projects like bio-gas plants, water preservation techniques, solar energy devices, etc., can be introduced for domestic use with a renewed sense of sustainability too. Local interfaith organizations or non-governmental organizations should be promoted for initiating such experiments.

A theological review of the theory of biological evolution can shed new light on the trajectory of science and religious interaction. This theory affirms a common origin of all forms of life and serves as a common ground for differences and diversity. Eastern religious traditions have immense resources, through which they can claim compatibility with the theory of evolution. The core of Hindu, Eastern Christian, and Buddhist philosophical thoughts are all in line with the evolution theory. These types of religious resources should be affirmed positively, not polemically or apologetically, and from a hospitality perspective. This new perspective of viewing biological evolution can have many positive consequences

---

27. Woloschak, "The Compatibility of the Principles," 213.

28. For example, the unethical/improper use of "endosulfan" in the cashew fields in Kasargod has caused severe health problems among the people over there. See Pulla, "Kerala's Endosulfan Tragedy."

on community life. In the Indian context, the hospitality aspect can promote meaningful interfaith relations, and science and religion dialogue, in a very practical way. I believe that authentic scientific expression should be complimented by ethical and religious resources. In the same way, an authentic religious experience should be enriched by scientific research and truths. The time has come for religion and science to *hear each other, and heal each other*!

Chapter 11

Eco-spiriting our Religious Philosophies
On Reviewing the Ecospirit[1]

ECOSPIRIT IS A BEAUTIFUL anthology of eco-spirited essays from a broad spectrum of interdisciplinary themes. It calls attention to new sets of questions and challenges in the field of eco-theology. The focal point of the work is reclaiming a common ground for the planetary existence in the context of an impending ecological "tipping point." A re-grounding of philosophical, theological, and religious resources is attempted in the book so that we can make a "green shift" for a sustainable future. For this purpose, the "trans-disciplinary collective"[2] re-theorizes (de-theorizes) the "nature/environment," which has been negatively influenced by conceptual backdrops of both Platonic dualism and the European enlightenment.

The context in which the eminent work fleshes out is well-explained by the co-editors, Catherine Keller and Laurel Kearns, in the preface and introduction. The fundamental imperative behind this anthology is the impending climate change and its various

---

1. This article is a critical review of the following book: Kearns and Keller, *Ecospirit: Religions and Philosophies*, 644.
2. The collective of writers behind *Ecospirit: Religions and Philosophies*.

far-reaching effects. What roles do religion and philosophy play in supporting a green shift in the context of the ecological crisis? What are the pathologies and potentialities within these religious and philosophical resources? What type of coalitions and collaborations are plausible? *Ecospirit* tries to answer these kinds of significant questions. Another significant crisis that editors mention is "an apocalyptic exhaustion and collective depression"[3] affected in eco-theological engagements. We also must confront this feeling of lethargy for a future sustainable earth.

According to the "trans-disciplinary collective," the fundamental problem behind the ecological crisis is the lack of common ground and lack of theorizing the "environment" (nature) across academic disciplines. Thus, a re-grounding and re-theorizing of "environment" are needed. A shared common ground of the universe should be reclaimed. The totalizing and homogenizing tendencies of the Western notion of universality must be problematized as well. So the *Ecospirit* as a whole is an attempt to deconstruct and reconstruct the religious and philosophical resources for fostering a common sustainable future. The work is transdisciplinary in its approach.

The authors resolve this problem of under-theorizing and lack of common ground by reclaiming redemptive potentialities from various religious, spiritual, philosophical, theoretical, biblical, theological, and pragmatic resources to make inclusive solutions. The book calls for a renewed spirit of apocalyptic hope in the "small beginnings" of eco-spirited movements which can "precipitate a 'butterfly effect' of change, a tipping counterpoint, and an avalanche of responsible action."[4] The need to make deeper changes in the human outlook, especially the philosophical/spiritual transitions, is affirmed as well. In a nutshell, *Ecospirit* facilitates a culture of hope, new beginnings, and experimentations. All the essays share the spirit of hope, the spirit of difficulty, and the spirit of trans-disciplinarity in attempting for a "green shift."

---

3. Keller and Kearns, *Ecospirit: Religions and Philosophies*, 4.
4. Ibid., xi.

Eco-spiriting our Religious Philosophies

The essays in the book deconstruct dominant pietistic Christian ethics that focus on an other-worldly spirituality which negates the material experience of the world. Such dominant Christian ethics and eschatology result in the construction of denigrated earth and earthlings. These faulty epistemological presuppositions of the dominant Christian ethics and eschatology should be countered with the embodiment paradigms within the Biblical and religious traditions. The body/earth denigrating priorities of Christian ethics should be challenged and replaced with body/earth affirmative potentials which are encoded in the doctrines of creation, incarnation, and resurrection.

The authors have engaged with various philosophical and religious resources to make their argument for a common sustainable earthling future. The book is divided into six sections, with five or six articles in each section. The first section (Ecogrounds) deals with how the ecological concerns inspire inter-religious engagements and wider ecumenism. The second section (Econatures) includes significant essays on epistemological and theoretical issues. The third section (Econstructions) deals with the interface between theory and theology with particular reference to postmodern/poststructural sensibilities. The fourth section (Ecodoctrines) explores doctrinal nuances from the ecological perspective, with a special focus on pneumatology. The last two sections (Ecospaces and Ecohopes) deal with the themes of spatiality, hope, liturgy, architecture, and poetics.

Rhizomatic Multiplicity

The "rhizomatic move" in theory paved a revolutionary change in the ecological studies. Theoretically, the "rhizomatic origin" (popularized by Deleuze and Guattari in *A Thousand Plateaus)* calls for multiplicity, heterogeneity, and diversity of life. It deconstructs the homogenizing tendency, instead privileging multiplicity and plurivocity. The rhizomatic approach affirms "the movements—like grass or water lilies—in a transverse fashion across heterogeneous lines or patterns of structure."[5] The rhizomatic pattern cannot be traced back to a transcendental singular entity. This concept proposes an ecological interconnectedness, which does not reduce the many to one. Luke Higgins re-reads "dust" in the Genesis story as "Spirit-dust" from a rhizomatic sensibility. He develops a micropneumatology grounded on the rhizomatic principle of interconnectedness. He says: "we are connected to and responsible for one another not because we are all children of a higher/metaphysical God or common descendants on a single genealogical tree, but because we are all composed of the same creative Spirit-dust."[6]

Planetarity

"Planetarity" is another focal theme in *Ecospirit*. Inspired by the postcolonial theorists like Gayatri Chakravorty Spivak, Keller and Kearns use and elaborate the celebrated postcolonial theme "planetarity." For Spivak, "Planetarity" is a "limiting idea to counteract the global reach of capital and the computerized globe."[7] Spivak uses "planetarity" to critique globalization and its impacts. With an ecological sensibility, Keller and Kearns elaborate the concept "Planetarity" as the protection of the earth's "vitality, diversity and beauty."[8] It is a sense of "terrestrial trust" for them.

Ecosocial Metamorphosis

"Ecosocial metamorphosis"[9] is another important common thread in this volume. "Ecosocial metamorphosis" means the process of transcending religious and philosophical traditions into ecosocially relevant resources, through the facilitation of an ongoing negotiation between them. It is "to disclose various religious

---

5. Ibid., 255.
6. Ibid., 262.
7. Spivak, *Death of a Discipline*, 12.
8. Keller and Kearns, *Ecospirit*, 3.
9. Ibid., 5.

pathologies as well as redemptive potentialities."[10] This is very relevant in biblical hermeneutics. For example, the parochial/individualistic interpretation of "love" (John 3:16, "God so loved this world"/*the cosmos*) can be reinterpreted as the God's redemptive love towards the whole creation. Love then challenges us as an ecological vocation.

Ecospirit moves beyond the usual anthologies of ecological meditations. The book creates a "third space" of hope and faith in the midst of impending ecological crisis. It is a book of hope. It proposes a tipping *counter*point by engendering apocalyptic hope and faith into eco-spirited micro practices. It firmly believes in the "butterfly effect" of micro-engagements and alternative practices. The book employs a trans-disciplinary approach by transcending various disciplinary boundaries through bridging philosophy and theology, theory and practice, and walk and talk. And it challenges the reader to reposition herself/himself with a renewed sense of self and the "other."

10. Ibid.

Chapter 12

Reformation as 'Dangerous Memory'
Re-membering an unfinished Business.

Memories are not simply a matter of looking backward "archeologically," but future-oriented "forward memories.[1]

—Johann Baptist Metz

Johann Baptist Metz is one of the prominent theologians of the twentieth century, who deeply reflected upon the concept of 'memory' and pointed out the theological significance of the category. According to Metz, 'memory is not a counterpart to hope, leading us deceptively away from the risks of the future rather they are 'dangerous' and make demands on us.'[2] There are different kinds of memories. In some memories, the past is not taken seriously enough. In such memories, the past becomes a paradise without danger, a refuge from our present disappointment. There is another kind of memories, which bathes everything from the

---

1. Johannes Baptist Metz, *Faith in History and Society : Toward a Practical Fundamental Theology* (New York : Seabury Press, 1980), 109
2. Ibid.

past in a soft, conciliatory light! For example; an event of old soldiers exchange war yarns at a regimental dinner. In such memories of the war, war as an inferno is obliterated. The past is being filtered in these types of memories, and then memory can quickly become a 'false consciousness' of our past and an opiate for our present. But there is another form of memory, which makes demands on us! In this kind of memory, the past breaks through to the centerpoint of our lives and reveal new and dangerous insights for the present. For Metz, this kind of memories are the memories that we have to take into account, as they are 'dangerous,'in a theological sense of its missional demands with an incredible future content. I would like to re-read the reformation in the Malankara Church as a 'dangerous memory,' in the light of Metzian appropriation of the category. Of course, the event of reformation is a vibrant memory that we re[-]member and retell always, and the event is not a mere show case-piece, as it is ever-demanding, open-ended, and unfinished with future content.

MEMORY OF A DISRUPTIVE EVENT

For Metz, the shortest definition for religion is constructive interruption or disruption. In many ways, the reformation movement in Malankara Church was interruptive and disruptive regarding its re-formative sensibilities. By replacing all de-formative faith and practices, dogmas and doctrines, hegemonic language system and texts, with re-formative faith, practices, and texts, the reformation movement initiated a new religious, spiritual and cultural renaissance in Kerala. P. Govinda Pillai comments on the reformation in the Malankara Church initiated by Abraham Malpan, as one of the initial stage of Kerala renaissance (*Kerala Navodthanam*). Undoubtedly, the reformation event reclaimed the re-formative potentiality of the Church. This helped the people to critically evaluate the role of the Church in the social process of nineteenth century Kerala.

AN 'OPEN' EVENT: CONTINUITIES AND DISCONTINUITIES

As an open-ended process, reformation never inaugurated an exclusive new Church in 1836. Even though the Church has learned many things from the teachings of CMS missionaries, the reformers didn't adopt the western form of worship or liturgy as such but insisted on continuing the oriental nature of it. The reformative tradition retained some continuities. For example, the apostolic tradition, Episcopacy, Liturgical tradition, Family faith practices, etc. Apostolic tradition is the line in which the Church defined itself. By retaining the apostolic tradition, the Church was reclaiming the apostolic succession, Independence, and identity beyond the ethnic and communal interpretation of the tradition. More over it placed itself in line with the tradition of the Early Church (Acts ch.4f) which was characterized by its openness, equality, and fellowship.

Of course, the reformation initiated discontinuities also. The Reformed Church always upheld its evangelical spirit, mission orientation, and social awareness. The evangelical spirit challenged the people to construct a 'self' founded on the scripture and a 'life' based on justice and equality. It empowered the church to initiate new mission ventures. The mission activities were the re-invention of the Church in relation to other communities. The Maramon convention was the real birth place of many missionary outreach programs. Owing to this missionary fervor and zeal, the Church initiated several organizations like Evangelistic Association, Sevika Sanghom, etc. The Reformation enabled the church to involve in meaningful social engagements too. The mediatory priesthood replaced by the representative one. Lay leadership was affirmed. New economic practice emerged within the Church by the practice of voluntary gifts. The Church survived by the voluntary contributions of the believers. Several new formative engagements and practices were initiated based on the Bible. The Reformation process was a celebration of such re-formative engagements and practices. To understand the affirmations of the Reformation we have to consider these continuities and discontinuities seriously.

AN UNFINISHED BUSINESS OF RE-FORMATION

Remembrance is always re-membering activity! By remembering the reformation event, we are re-membering ourselves into the unfinished business of the re-formation. The reformation cannot be underestimated as a museum piece or period piece; rather it should be understood as an ongoing, unfinished project. And it should not be interpreted as a mere fragment of our common history, rather as a frag-event, whose power still fragments and shatters all reified institutions. Through the reformative engagements, the Church remolded the social relations within the Church. This process moved in connection with the social shifts in the nineteenth century Kerala. The reconstruction of social relations within the church also intended a reformulation of the relationship between the Church and the society. The event was Biblically grounded, historically informed, socially engaged, and mission oriented. Considering reformation as a dangerous memory of celebrating re-formative engagements and practices, I would like to highlight few affirmations of the reformation.

The Quest for Language and Texts

Like the reformation in the western Church, the reformation in the Malankara Church is also intrinsically related to a linguistic turn. Vitor Westelle says that 'there is no great historical event that is not associated with a linguistic phenomenon.'[3] The reformation movement in the Malankara church owes its historical impact to the way in which it was able to incorporate the Malayalam language of the people into its political, religious, and cultural program expanding it, giving it a dynamic formation and a

---

3. Vítor Westhelle, *Transfiguring Luther : The Planetary Promise of Luther's Theology* (Eugene, Oregon : Cascade Books, 2016), 24.

public character. By translating and chanting the liturgy in common people's language, the reformation movement consciously opted for a 'heteroglossia.' Heteroglossia is a linguistic practice of allowing different voices to enter into the conversation. By using common people's language, the reformation movement was able to give expression to the imagination of the people long suppressed by the limits of the prevailing institutions and language system. The insurrection of the vernacular was the result of this heteroglossia-expression, in that sense, the reformation has a subaltern motive. The quest for the language and heteroglossia is a very important issue for the subaltern people in the mission fields and also in the diaspora communities. The translation of Taksa from Syriac to Malayalam can be understood as a symbolic expression of discarding the dominant caste discourse and construction of a dialogical space within the emerging Kerala nationality. The usage of Malayalam Bible and Malayalam Taksa in the worship services was a process of democratization of hermeneutic power. It granted a new hermeneutic potentiality to the people. Through the interpretation and exposition of the texts, the symbolic world of the everyday living was subjected to and challenged by the realm of transcendence.

Dialectical Interaction with the Tradition

The Reformation was an act of dialectical interaction with the tradition based on continuity and discontinuity dialectics, as mentioned earlier. It was a process of re-reading the epistemic routes of the traditions and re-forming the Church based on the Scripture, guided by the Holy Spirit. It is an ongoing process particularly in the mission fields of the Church today. How seriously we take the linguistic and cultural traditions of the communities in the mission fields is a challenging question. By engaging in the mission works, we are placing the church in a challenging space, so that it should be reformed again and again in the light of the 'dangerous memory' of reformation. How far we take the history, traditions, and culture of the Dalits, Traibals, Native Americans, and the

Mexicans in the light of this 'dangerous memory' of reformation is a significant concern in the multi-cultural context of the Mar Thoma Church today.

Reflexive Practices of Self-Formation

By rejecting meaningless cult practices like *Muthappan Chatham* and veneration of saints, Reformation affirmed meaningful reflexive faith practices of self-formation. The faith practices like Bible Reading, Preaching, Teaching, Family Prayer meetings, Public discourses like Conventions, Voluntary contributions, Voluntary evangelism, etc. made the church life meaningful. It was an event of making the Church 'real'. The formation of Organizations like Sevika Sanghom, Sunday School, etc. are the evidence of new meaningful engagements in the human formation. Such reflexive practices challenged the believers to engage meaningfully in the society.

Re-Imagined Ecclesia: Hyphenations

In sum, the reformation was a biblically grounded re-imagination the Church. It was a challenge to redefine the relations within the Church and outside the Church based on the kingdom values. Re-ordering the hierarchies within the Church and the society through the faith and practice was an essential thrust. The mission ventures of the Church helped to redefine its identity beyond communal exclusivism. The ecumenical relationship enabled the church to relate to other churches and join in the mission together. The most important characteristic of the Mar Thoma tradition is its hyphenated nature. The in-between / betwixt nature, or in other words the liminal character of the tradition makes it unique. The hyphens between, 'East—West,' 'traditional-reformed,' and 'Global-local' symbolically refer to the higher responsibility of the Church in doing its bridging mission. To keep this potential liminal character of the tradition, the

Church should de-institutionalize, re-position, and re-construct herself time to time.

DEMANDS OF THE 'DANGEROUS MEMORY'

The retelling of the 'dangerous memory' of the event of reformation, gifts us many demands. The demands are at least three levels, namely in Theological formulations, Ecclesiological re-imaginations, and Missiological aspirations. The Church should engage in active contextual-theological-formulations grounded on the continuities and discontinuities of the Reformation. In other words, the Reformation tradition must be theologically interpreted and affirmed time to time. The 'memory' must be retold in the perspectives of women, Dalits, and the marginalized. The Church should continue its reformation spirit by meaningful formative engagements and practices. The Church has to equip the people with a hermeneutic capacity to realize how they should participate in the social process. Affirmation of Laity is the spirit of Reformation. Keeping the critical awareness and hermeneutic capacity of the people is important. An integral relationship between the Alter-Pulpit-People relationship should be emphasized. The formation through the liturgical practices should be affirmed. The mission activities should not end up with the construction of the 'margins' or 'others.' It is the time to realize that, the margins are not the fragile spaces, but it is where the fragility of the church is manifested.

Westhelle reminds us that, the spirit of the Reformation can be quickly hardened to the institutional patterns. [4] How far we can keep the spirit of reformation is depended upon how far we able to keep church as an event not as a convenient institution. Keeping the liminal character, and the missional momentum of the Church is very significant in keeping the Church ever renewing. As a 'dangerous memory,' the Reformation always demands deconstruction, and reconstruction of the very nature of the

4. Ibid., 3.

Church grounded on faith, scripture, and with the guidance of the Holy Spirit. The church always should be like a river, that ever-flowing, ever-renewing, and ever-refreshing. Like the river renews itself through its constant connectivity with its source, the Church should be renewed by the power of the holy spirit, reconnecting and re-membering its calling and election, manifested in the historical event of reformation. Let me conclude by reminiscing the words of Walter Brueggemann, 'Church is not accidental, it is radically intentional.'

Bibliography

Agamben, Giorgio. *The Coming Community*. Translated by Michael Hardt. Minneapolis: University of Minnesota Press, 1993.
———. *Homo Sacer: Sovereign Power and Bare Life*. Translated by Daniel Heller-Roazen. Stanford: Stanford University Press, 1998.
———. *The Time That Remains: A Commentary on the Letter to the Romans*. Stanford: Stanford University Press, 2005.
Apffel-Marglin, Frederique, and Pramod Parajuli. "'Sacred Grove' and Ecology: Ritual and Science." In *Hinduism and Ecology: The Intersection of Earth, Sky, and Water*, edited by Christopher Key Chapple, et. al. Massachusetts: Harvard University Press, 2000.
Arnold, Daniel Anderson. *Buddhists, Brahmins, and Belief Epistemology in South Asian Philosophy of Religion*. New York: Columbia University Press, 2005.
Bhabha, Homi K. *The Location of Culture*. London and New York: Routledge, 1994.
Bachelard, Gaston, and John R. Stilgoe. *The Poetics of Space*. Translated by Maria Jolas. Reprint edition. Boston: Beacon, 1994.
Bagir, Zainal Abidin. *Science and Religion in a Post-Colonial World: Interfaith Perspectives*. Science and Theology Series 8. Adelaide, Australia: ATF, 2005.
Bahloul, Joelle. *The Architecture of Memory: A Jewish-Muslim Household in Colonial Algeria, 1937–1962*. New York: Cambridge University Press, 1996.
Bateson, Mary Catherine. *Peripheral Visions: Learning Along the Way*. New York: Harper Collins, 1994.
Baudrillard, Jean. *Impossible Exchange*. London: Verso, 2001.
Bearn, Gordon C. *Life Drawing: A Deleuzean Aesthetics of Existence*. New York: Fordham University Press, 2013.

Bibliography

Bell, Catherine. *Ritual Theory, Ritual Practice*. New York: Oxford University Press, 1992.

———. *Ritual: Perspectives and Dimensions*. New York: Oxford University Press, 1997.

Benjamin, Walter. *Illuminations: Essays and Reflections*. New York: Schocken, 2007.

Bhatt, Chandi Prasad. "Chipko Movement: The Hug That Saves." In *Hindu Survey of the Environment*. Madras, India: The Hindu National Press, 1991.

Borde, Radhika. "The Devi as Ecofeminist Warrior: Reclaiming the Role of Sacred Natural Sites in East-Central India." In *Sacred Natural Sites: Conserving Nature and Culture*, 272–9. London: Routledge, 2010.

Brown, C. Mackenzie. *The Triumph of the Goddess: The Canonical Models and Theological Visions of the Devi-Bhagavata Purana*. New York: SUNY, 1990.

Bulgakov, Sergius. *The Bride of the Lamb*. Grand Rapids, MI: W. B. Eerdmans, 2002.

Buxhoeveden, Daniel, and Gayle Woloschak. *Science and the Eastern Orthodox Church*. Burlington, VT: Ashgate, 2011.

Cage, John. *Silence*. Middletown, CT: Wesleyan University Press, 1973.

Capra, Fritjof. *The Tao of Physics: An Exploration of the Parallels Between Modern Physics and Eastern Mysticism*. Berkeley, CA: Shambhala, 1975.

Clarke, Sathianathan. *Dalits and Christianity: Subaltern Religion and Liberation Theology in India*. New Delhi, India: Oxford University Press, 2000.

———. "Subaltern Culture as Resource for People's Liberation: A Critical Inquiry into Dalit Cultural Theory." *Religion and Society* 44, no. 4 (December 1997) 84–105.

Cohen, Signe. *Text and Authority in the Older Upaniṣads*. Brill's Indological Library. Boston: Brill, 2008.

Crossely, Nick. "Ritual, Body Technique and (Inter) Subjectivity." In *Thinking Through Rituals: Philosophical Perspectives*, edited by Kevin Schrilbrack. London: Routledge, 2004.

Darwin, Charles. *On the Origin of Species by Means of Natural Selection or the Preservation of Favored Races in the Struggle for Life and the Descent of Man and Selection in Relation to Sex*. New York: Random House, 1936.

Deleuze, Gilles, and Felix Guattari. *A Thousand Plateaus: Capitalism and Schizophrenia*. Minneapolis: University of Minnesota Press, 1987.

Devasahayam, V. *Dalits & Women: Quest for Humanity*. Tamilnadu, India: Gurukul Lutheran Theological College & Research Institute (UELC), 1992.

Dickinson, Colby. *Agamben and Theology*. New York: T & T Clark, 2011.

Dobzhansky, Theodosius. *Mankind Evolving: The Evolution of the Human Species*. New Haven: Yale University Press, 1967.

Douglas, Kelly Brown. *The Black Christ*. Maryknoll, NY: Orbis, 1994.

———. *What's Faith Got to Do with It? Black Bodies/Christian Souls*. Maryknoll, NY: Orbis Books, 2005.

Bibliography

Dwivedi, O. P. "Dharmic Ecology." In *Hinduism and Ecology*. Massachusetts: Harvard University Press, 2000.

Edelmann, Jonathan B. *Hindu Theology and Biology: The Bhagavata Purana and Contemporary Theory*. Oxford: Oxford Theology and Religion Monographs, 2012.

Edgerton, Franklin. *The Bhagavad Gita: Translated and Interpreted by Franklin Edgerton*. Cambridge: Harvard University Press, 1944.

Esposito, Roberto, and Vanessa Lemm. *Terms of the Political: Community, Immunity, Biopolitics*. Translated by Rhiannon Noel Welch. 1st edition. New York: Fordham University Press, 2012.

Falzon, Christopher. *Foucault and Social Dialogue: Beyond Fragmentation*. New York: Routledge, 1998.

Foucault, Michel. *The Archaeology of Knowledge*. London: Routledge, 1972.

Fox, Matthew. *The Coming of the Cosmic Christ: The Healing of Mother Earth and the Birth of a Global Renaissance*. San Francisco: Harper & Row, 1988.

Frazer, James George. *The Golden Bough: A Study in Magic and Religion*. New York: The Macmillan Co., 1935.

Gadgil, Madhav, and Ramachandra Guha. *This Fissured Land: An Ecological History of India*. Berkeley: University of California Press, 1993.

———, and V. D. Vartak. "Sacred Groves of India: A Plea for Continued Conservation 72 (1975): 314–20." *The Journal of the Bombay Natural History Society* 72 (1975) 314–20.

George, P. T. "The Promised Land: Adivasi Land Struggles in Kerala-Ritimo." http://www.ritimo.org/The-Promised-Land-Adivasi-Land-Struggles-in-Kerala.

George, Sunny. "Study." In *Re-Imagining Dalit Theology: Postmodern Readings*, by Y. T. Vinaya Raj, 13-15. Thiruvalla, India: CSS, 2010.

Guha, Ranajit, ed. Preface to *Subaltern Studies: Writings on South Asian History and Society*, vol. 1. New Delhi: Oxford University Press, 1997.

Gyatso, Geshe Kelsang. *Joyful Path of Good Fortune: The Complete Buddhist Path to Enlightenment*. 2nd ed. Glen Spey, NY: Tharpa Publications, 1995.

Harink, Douglas. *Paul, Philosophy, and the Theopolitical Vision: Critical Engagements with Agamben, Badiou, Zizek, and Others*. Eugene, OR: Wipf & Stock, 2010.

Heidegger, Martin. *Being and Time*. Translated by Joan Stambaugh. Revised edition. Albany: State University of New York Press, 2010.

Highland, Chris. *Meditations of Henry David Thoreau: A Light in the Woods*. Berkeley: Wilderness Press, 2010.

Hopkins, Dwight N., and Linda E. Thomas, eds. *Walk Together Children: Black and Womanist Theologies, Church and Theological Education*. Eugene, OR: Wipf & Stock, 2010.

Horsfjord, Vebjørn L. "Challenging Contexts: A Study of Two Contemporary Indian Christian Theologians and a Reflection on the Need for Intercontextual Dialogue." *Studia Theologica* 55, no. 1 (2001) 41–57.

Jensen, Alexander. *Theological Hermeneutics*. London: SCM, 2007.

Bibliography

"Kammatipaadam." *Wikipedia*. https://en.wikipedia.org/w/index.php?title=Kammatipaadam&oldid=748289100.

Kang, Namsoon. *Cosmopolitan Theology*. St. Louis: Chalice, 2013.

Kant, Immanuel. *Critique of Pure Reason*. Reprint. London: Cambridge University Press, 1999.

Kapikkad, Sunny. "Thiraskritharude Charisthram: Bhashanavum Yukthiyum." Kottayam, India: Unpublished, 2004.

Kearney, Richard. "Epiphanies of the Everyday: Toward a Micro-Eschatology." In *After God: Richard Kearney and the Religious Turn in Continental Philosophy*, 3–20. New York: Fordham University Press, 2006.

———, and Jens Zimmermann, eds. *Reimagining the Sacred: Richard Kearney Debates God*. New York: Columbia University Press, 2015.

Kearns, Laurel, and Catherine Keller. *Ecospirit: Religions and Philosophies for the Earth*. New York: Fordham University Press, 2007.

Kent, Eliza F. *Sacred Groves and Local Gods Religion and Environmentalism in South India*. New York: Oxford University Press, 2013.

Kumar, Ajith. "An Ethnographic Violence." *Campus Alive*. http://campusalive.in/kammattipadamanethnographicviolence/.

Laird, Sarah A. "Trees, Forests and Sacred Groves." In *The Overstory Book: Cultivating Connections with Trees*, 30–34. Holualoa: Permanent Agriculture Resources, 2004.

Larson, Gerald. "Karma as a 'Sociology of Knowledge' or 'Social Psychology' of Process/Praxis." In *Karma and Rebirth in Classical Indian Traditions*, edited by Wendy Doniger O'Flaherty, 303–316. Berkely: University of California Press, 1980.

Lazzarato, Maurizio. *The Making of the Indebted Man: An Essay on the Neoliberal Condition*. Los Angeles: Semiotext(e), 2012.

Levinas, Emmanuel. *Difficult Freedom: Essays on Judaism*. Baltimore, MD: The Johns Hopkins University Press, 1990.

Lincoln, Bruce. *Discourse and the Construction of Society Comparative Studies of Myth, Ritual, and Classification*. New York: Oxford University Press, 1989.

Lyotard, Jean-Francois, and Fredric Jameson. *The Postmodern Condition: A Report on Knowledge*. Translated by Geoff Bennington and Brian Massumi. 1st edition. Minneapolis: University Of Minnesota Press, 1984.

Maathai, Wangari. *The Green Belt Movement: Sharing the Approach and the Experience*. Revised edition. New York: Lantern Books, 2003.

"Mahatma Gandhi." *Wikiquote*. https://en.wikiquote.org/wiki/Mahatma_Gandhi.

Malayalienter. "Kammatti Paadam Movie Review Ft. Dulquer Salmaan, Vinayakan, Rajeev Ravi." https://www.youtube.com/watch?v=6WXqrg9bAII.

Maniyath, Jithesh. "Forests of Belief." *Kerala Calling* 26, no. 2 (February 2006) 28–32.

BIBLIOGRAPHY

Manoussakis, John Panteleimon. *After God: Richard Kearney and the Religious Turn in Continental Philosophy.* 1st edition. New York: Fordham University Press, 2006.
Mantzaridis, Georgios I. *The Deification of Man.* Crestwood: St. Vladimir Seminary, 1984.
Mar Gregorios, Paulos. *The Human Presence: Ecological Spirituality and the Age of the Spirit.* New York: Amity House, 1987.
———. *A Light Too Bright.* Albany: State University of New York Press, 1992.
Marglin, Frederique Apffel, and Pramod Parajuli. "'Sacred Grove' and Ecology: Ritual and Science." In *Hinduism and Ecology.* Cambridge, MA: Harvard University Press, 2000.
McKenna, Josephine. "Pope Francis: 'Evolution . . . Is Not Inconsistent with the Notion of Creation.'" *Religion News Service.* http://www.religionnews.com/2014/10/27/pope-francis-evolution-inconsistent-notion-creation/.
Metz, Johannes Baptist. *Faith in History and Society: Toward a Practical Fundamental Theology.* New York: Seabury, 1980.
Mignolo, Walter D. *Local Histories/Global Designs: Coloniality, Subaltern Knowledges, and Border Thinking.* Princeton, NJ: Princeton University Press, 2000.
Mills, Sara. *Michel Foucault.* 1st edition. New York: Routledge, 2003.
Mohan, Sanal P. *Modernity of Slavery.* New Delhi: Oxford University Press, 2015.
Nagarajan, Saraswathy. "How Green was My City." *The Hindu.* http://www.thehindu.com/features/cinema/How-GREEN-was-my-city/article14380296.ece.
Nagarajan, Vijaya. "Rituals of Embedded Ecologies: Drawing Kolams, Marrying Trees, and Generating Auspiciousness." In *Hinduism and Ecology,* edited by Christopher Key Chapple, et. al., 453–68. Cambridge, MA: Harvard University Press, 2000.
Nietzsche, Friedrich. *On the Genealogy of Morals and Ecce Homo.* Edited by Walter Kaufmann. Reissue edition. New York: Vintage, 1989.
Olivelle, Patrick, trans. *The Early Upanishads: Annotated Text and Translation.* New York: Oxford University Press, 1998.
———, trans. *Upaniṣads.* Oxford: Oxford University Press, 2008.
Omvedt, Gail. *Seeking Begumpura: The Social Vision of Anticaste Intellectuals.* New Delhi, India: Navayana, 2008.
Oommen, M. A. *Land Reforms and Socio-Economic Change in Kerala: An Introductory Study.* Madras: Christian Literature Society, 1971.
Parayil, Sujith Kumar. "Visual Perception and Cultural Memory: Typecast and Typecast(e)ing in Malayalam Cinema." *SYNOPTIQUE: An Online Journal of Film and Moving Image Studies* 3, no. 1 (May 8, 2014) 67–98.
Pillai, Elamkulam Kunjan. *Jenmi Systems in Kerala.* Kottayam: National Book Stall, 1966.
Pollock, Sheldon. "Mīmāṃsā and the Problem of History in Traditional India." *Journal of the American Oriental Society* 109, no. 4 (October 1989) 603–10.

Bibliography

Pulla, Priyanka. "Kerala's Endosulfan Tragedy." *OPEN Magazine*. http://www.openthemagazine.com/article/nation/kerala-s-endosulfan-tragedy.

Raj, Riya Jez. "Childhood Stories: The Guard of Waynad Churam-Karinthandan." *Childhood Stories*, November 1, 2012. http://tuhinastories.blogspot.com/2012/11/the-guard-of-wayanad-churam-karnthandan.html.

Rajpal, Harish. "Dasavatar—Ten Avatars of Lord Vishnu." http://srisrimadbhagavatamkatha.blogspot.com/2012/11/dasavatar-ten-avatars-of-lord-vishnu.html.

Raman, Varadaraja V. "Traditional Hinduism and Modern Science." In *Bdidging Science and Religion*, 1st edition, 185–95. London: SCM Press, 2009.

Robinson, Andrew. "In Theory: Giorgio Agamben: Destroying Sovereignty." Ceasefire Magazine. https://ceasefiremagazine.co.uk/in-theory-giorgio-agamben-destroying-sovereignty/.

Rogers-Vaughn, Bruce. *Caring for Souls in a Neoliberal Age*. Nashville: Palgrave Macmillan, 2016.

Rosenthal, Gilbert S. "Tikkun Ha-Olam: The Metamorphosis of a Concept." *The Journal of Religion* 85, no. 2 (April 2005) 214–40.

Rowena, Jenny. "Locating P K Rosy: Can A Dalit Woman Play a Nair Role in Malayalam Cinema Today?" http://www.dalitweb.org/?p=1641.\.

Sahi, Jyothi. "Seeds of Tradition." *Journal of Dharma* 23, no. 1 (March 1998) 95.

"Sarnaism." *Wikipedia*. https://en.wikipedia.org/wiki/Sarnaism.

Schleiermacher, Friedrich. *Hermeneutics : The Handwritten Manuscripts*. Missoula, MT: Scholars, 1977.

Selected Hymns and Order of Worship. 53rd ed. Thiruvalla, India: Mar Thoma Sabha Publication Board, 2012.

Shaye, Amaryah. "Blackness and Value; Part 3: On Blackness as Debt." https://womenintheology.org/2015/03/02/blackness-and-value-part-3-on-blackness-as-debt/.

Shepherd, Andrew. *The Gift of the Other: Levinas, Derrida, and a Theology of Hospitality*. Eugene, Oregon: Pickwick, 2014.

Shiva, Vandana. *Staying Alive: Women, Ecology, and Development*. New Delhi: Zed Books, 1988.

Spivak, Gayatri Chakravorty. *Death of a Discipline*. New York: Columbia University Press, 2005.

———. "Subaltern Studies: Deconstructing Historiography." In *Subaltern Studies IV: Writings on South Asian History and Society*, vol. 1., edited by Ranajit Guha. New Delhi: Oxford University Press, 1997.

Thilly, Frank. *A History of Philosophy*. Allahabad: Central Publishing House, 1996.

Thomas, Linda E. *Under the Canopy : Ritual Process and Spiritual Resilience in South Africa*. Columbia, SC: University of South Carolina Press, 1999.

Thurman, Howard. *Jesus and the Disinherited*. New York: Abingdon-Cokesbury, 1949.

Bibliography

Trivedi, Divya. "The Butterfly Effect." http://www.thehindu.com/features/cinema/the-butterfly-effect/article3954653.ece.

Van Wieren, Gretel. *Restored to Earth: Christianity, Environmental Ethics, and Ecological Restoration*. Washington, DC: Georgetown University Press, 2013.

Vanier, Jean. *Community and Growth*. New York: Paulist, 1989.

Vinayaraj, Y. T. "Ecclesiology with(out) Margins: Defining Church in the Context of Empire." *The Asia Journal of Theology* 30, no. 1 (April 2016) 79–95.

———. "Envisioning a Postmodern Method of Doing Dalit Theology." In *Dalit Theology in the Twenty-First Century: Discordant Voices, Discerning Pathways*, 93–103. New Delhi: Oxford University Press, 2010.

———. *Re-Visiting the Other: Discourses on Postmodern Theology*. Thiruvalla, India: CSS, 2010.

Walker, Alice. *In Search of Our Mothers' Gardens*. Orlando, FL: Harcourt, 2004.

Watkin, William. *Agamben and Indifference: A Critical Overview*. Lanham: Rowman & Littlefield International, 2013.

Weber, Max. *The Protestant Ethic and the Spirit of Capitalism*. 2nd edition. New York: Routledge, 2001.

Westhelle, Vítor. *Eschatology and Space: The Lost Dimension in Theology Past and Present*. New York: Palgrave Macmillan, 2012.

———. *Transfiguring Luther: The Planetary Promise of Luther's Theology*. Eugene, OR: Cascade, 2016.

Williams, Maxine. "Black Women and Struggle for Liberation." http://library.duke.edu/Rubenstein/scriptorium/wlm/blkmanif/

Woloschak, Gayle E. *Beauty and Unity in Creation: The Evolution of Life*. Minneapolis, Minn: Light & Life Publishing, 1996.

———. "The Compatibility of the Principles of Biological Evolution with Eastern Orthodoxy." *St Vladimir's Theological Quarterly* 55, no. 2 (January 1, 2011) 209–31.

Zuesse, Evan M. *Ritual Cosmos*. Athens, OH: Ohio University Press, 1985.

www.ingramcontent.com/pod-product-compliance
Lightning Source LLC
Chambersburg PA
CBHW072150160426
43197CB00012B/2329